Friends of Jesus

Colin Urquhart has been in Christian ministry for well over 30 years. He was a leading figure in the charismatic movement, while an Anglican minister. For the last 20 years he has travelled world-wide, speaking in over 40 nations, mostly at national and international conferences.

During this period he has been Director of Kingdom Faith Ministries and is also Senior Pastor of Kingdom Faith Church, based at the National Revival Centre, Horsham, West Sussex, a rapidly expanding church with a widespread influence encouraging revival among several nations.

Colin is married to Caroline who has shared with him the triumphs and trials of a long ministry. They have three children – Claire, Clive and Andrea – all of whom are involved in ministry.

Friends of Jesus

Colin Urquhart

Marshall Pickering
An Imprint of HarperCollins*Publishers*

Marshall Pickering is an Imprint of
HarperCollins*Religious*

Part of HarperCollins*Publishers*
77–85 Fulham Palace Road, London W6 8JB

First published in 1997 by
HarperCollins*Publishers*

1 3 5 7 9 10 8 6 4 2

A catalogue record for this book is
available from the British Library

0 551 031158

Printed and bound in Great Britain by
Caledonian International Book Manufacturing Ltd,
Glasgow

To all those who decide to live
as the Friends of Jesus

Thank You

My grateful thanks to the Lord for the vision of Friends of Jesus International. I pray that God will use this to bring Christians together in love and unity to be more effective in their witness to the world of the truth and power of the Gospel.

I am grateful to my wife, Caroline, for her loving support. Thanks also to Paula, my assistant, for her many hours of help and encouragement in producing this book, and to all at Kingdom Faith who share with me the vision of the Friends of Jesus.

The biblical quotations are from the New International Version, except where indicated. NLT stands for the New Living Translation.

Note

You may like to read through this book to obtain an overview of what it means to live as a Friend of Jesus.

However, most benefit will be obtained by reading one of the short chapters each day and then praying the brief prayer at the end of each chapter. Repeat the prayer several times during the course of the day so that it becomes your own.

Contents

He Wants You As His Friend

Only a few hours previously He had called them His friends. Since then, instead of praying during His time of greatest need, they had fallen asleep! When He was arrested they had all fled, leaving Him alone. One of them had even denied three times that he knew Him! Later they could only stand by and watch Him hanging on a cross, powerless to help Him. What friends!

After His death they met together, their dreams shattered. News came from some of the women that He had risen from the dead. Even though He had predicted this on a number of occasions, they had neither understood nor believed Him. When two others said they had seen Him, they still did not believe. What faith!

And yet these men were those Jesus had specially selected to establish the Church and turn the world upside down! These were the friends of Jesus!

Jesus wants **you** as His friend. This may seem as strange a choice as those original friends. Their weakness and failure are enshrined in Scripture for all to read. What a bunch: fishermen, a former tax-collector, a zealot, a few nobodies and one renowned for his unbelief!

So why not **you**? Think of what those men became, despite their inadequacies! They had the privilege of walking with Jesus, not only in the flesh, not only in His risen body, but even more wonderfully, in the Spirit.

This is the same walk Jesus intends for you as a Christian, that you relate to Him as a close friend, with His Spirit living in you to enable you to do all He asks of you.

How can such things be, knowing your inadequacies so clearly? Do you imagine you will follow the example of your biblical predecessors and fail dismally?

What is the alternative? That you say to Jesus, 'I don't want to be your friend'? Can you really expect to have Him as your Friend if you are not prepared to be His friend? Isn't friendship something that has to be mutual?

If Jesus has chosen you, He has chosen you for a friend! Is this the first mistake He has ever made, to say to you, 'I want you for my friend'? Did He come to the wrong address when He called you? Surely He knew what He was taking on when He first chose you. Yes, you were His own deliberate choice! Why? **Because He values you so highly, He wants you as His friend now and for all eternity!**

When writing to 'all Christians everywhere', Paul said:

> He always does just what he says, and he is the one who invited you into this wonderful friendship with his Son, Jesus Christ our Lord. (1 Corinthians 1:9; NLT)

How can you respond to such a call? How could you be a loving and faithful friend, even though like Peter, John and the others, there may be many times when you fail in your friendship?

These are the questions we are going to address. The answers will encourage you, for you will see that it is possible to live as a friend of Jesus and know that He enables you to fulfil the plan and purpose He has for your life.

Prayer: *Lord Jesus, I want to live as your friend.*

Two

The First Friends

'Come follow me.' Were those the first words Jesus had addressed personally to those four fishermen by the Sea of Galilee? Whether they were or not, they were enough for those men to take the decision to leave everything and follow Him. Perhaps He spoke with such love and authority that they knew He was not to be denied. Certainly, He gave them no job description or promises, beyond the fact that He would make them fishers of men, whatever He meant by that!

The following months must have been both wondrous and exciting for them. Nobody had ever spoken like this man, or taught with such authority. And then there were all the healings and other miracles that were taking place. It must have seemed as if they had suddenly been transported into another dimension spiritually.

Jesus had a variety of relationships. He related to the crowds at one level, the thousands who flocked to hear Him preach and teach, who longed to see the miracles He performed.

He had a wide circle of followers or disciples. Of these we know nothing in detail – the seventy He sent out, the five hundred to whom He appeared in His risen body. Jesus had a number of much closer relationships. He had a distinctive relationship with the twelve disciples, including Judas who was to betray Him. Within His intimate circles of friends, three had a particularly close relationship with Him: Peter, James and John.

Jesus made it clear to His disciples that they were special to Him. He would make time to be alone with them, even though the people clamoured for His attention. He would explain things to them that the crowd could not understand.

However, Jesus had other close friends, not numbered in the twelve disciples. There was the family at Bethany, Mary, Martha and Lazarus, whom He raised from the dead. Mary Magdalene was given the privilege of being the first person to see Him after His resurrection. There was the group of women that followed Him around on His missions, to care for His needs. Little is said about them or the way in which they related to Him, but they were with Him as His friends.

And, of course, there was His mother. His love and care for her was shown on the cross when He entrusted her to John's care, and from that time John took her into his home.

Jesus thought of His friends as part of His family. There was an occasion when His mother and brothers came looking for Him, but could not get near because of the crowd listening to Him. So they passed a message forward to Jesus: 'Your mother and brothers are standing outside, wanting to speak to you.' To this Jesus replied:

'Who is my mother, and who are my brothers?' Pointing to his disciples, he said, 'Here are my mother and brothers. For whoever does the will of my Father in heaven is my brother and sister and mother.'
(Matthew 12:47–50)

This is a radical new concept of family! His disciples are part of His family because they do His Father's will! Yet they certainly did not succeed in being obedient always. They often failed Jesus even though their hearts were set on pleasing Him, on living to fulfil God's purpose for their lives. **He did not condemn them for their failures; He was infinitely patient with them.**

The Lord is infinitely patient with us, also.

Prayer: *Lord Jesus, thank you for being patient with me and for not condemning me for my failures.*

☙

Three

Rich in Love

> The Lord is gracious and compassionate, slow to anger
> and rich in love. (Psalm 145:8)

If God was to deal with man as he deserved, He would
wipe him from the face of the earth in judgement. For sin
is so deeply offensive to the Lord, who is holy, pure and un-
defiled, that it renders us worthy only of condemnation,
death and eternal separation from Him.

Before we could be acceptable in His sight, someone had
to suffer for us the condemnation and death we deserve;
someone like us in every way, except that He did not sin!
God couldn't say that sin didn't matter because it had
brought about a great barrier between God and His people.
This barrier could only be removed through the offering of
a perfect life for the imperfect, a sinless life offered to God
on behalf of sinners, a righteous offering on behalf of the
unrighteous.

Sin had deprived sinners of the glory for which God had
created them.

Nobody could hold up his good works before His judgement seat and expect to enter heaven on the basis of what
he had done. There was not one person anywhere who
could deserve to have a relationship with God, or to be part
of His heaven.

No one but Jesus could offer to God a sinless offering.
Nobody else could come to Him because of his or her own

efforts or godliness. No one could make any claim on Him on the basis of what he or she had accomplished.

And so God Himself provided the sacrifice. He sent His Son, Jesus, who did what no other man has ever done or could ever do: He lived the perfect, sinless life. He lived in perfect love, in perfect obedience to the Father.

He revealed His Father's love, not only through the things He taught, but by the kind of person He was, and the things He did. Jesus had only one aim: to do the will of His Father. He lived in a relationship of such love with His Father that He could say, 'The Father and I are One.' And, 'If you have seen me you have seen the Father.'

> He is the image of the invisible God, the firstborn over all creation … For God was pleased to have all his fullness dwell in him, and through him to receive to himself all things, whether things on earth or things in heaven, by making peace through his blood, shed on the cross. (Colossians 1:15, 19–20)

The work of reconciling men to God, of restoring man to unity with Him in a relationship of genuine love, could only be accomplished by God alone. He had to provide the sinless sacrifice that would enable us to be forgiven and reconciled to God.

> Behold, the lamb of God who takes away the sin of the world. (John 1:29)

Jesus had to share our human frailty and weakness, be subjected to every temptation we experience, and yet still remain without sin, faithful and obedient to the Father. He could not be a valid sacrifice on our behalf unless He was in every way human like us, but without sin!

Because in love for His Father He lived the life of perfect obedience and submission, He could take on Himself all the sins that would result from our disobedience and rebellion against His authority.

> He was pierced for our transgressions, he was crushed for our iniquities; the punishment that brought us peace was upon him, and by his wounds we are healed.
> (Isaiah 53:5)

Not only did He take our sins, He suffered the punishment we deserve so that we could be set free from the consequences of our sins and have peace with God.

> We all, like sheep, have gone astray, each of us has turned to his own way; and the Lord has laid on Him the iniquity of us all. (Isaiah 53:6)

We deserve judgement. But Jesus had come not to judge and condemn, but to save and heal! **He had not come to give us what we deserve, but to reveal the nature of God's wonderful love for us.**

You need never question that love. He has already demonstrated the full extent of His love in sending Jesus to die for you. He took all your sin, guilt and shame upon Himself. He suffered on your behalf the punishment you deserve, and instead lets you go free.

He has shown His wonderful mercy in forgiving you all your sins, in cleansing you completely and making you acceptable to Him through Jesus. You could never make yourself acceptable, but your faith in Jesus saves you from the condemnation you deserved.

> For God so loved the world that he gave his one and
> only Son, that whoever believes in him shall not perish
> but have eternal life. For God did not send his Son into
> the world to condemn the world, but to save the world
> through him. (John 3:16–17)

As a believer in Jesus Christ, not only does God forgive
you, He gives you eternal life, His life. You have been reconciled with God and so can know the wonder of His grace
in giving you all the blessings of His Kingdom.

You have been made one with Christ, who is one with
the Father. Now you can live in the love of Jesus. And His
love can live in you. For God, the Holy Spirit, lived in Jesus
during His humanity and comes to live in the humanity of
every born-again Christian.

> Our fellowship is with the Father and with his Son, Jesus
> Christ. (1 John 1:3)

Fellowship is the sharing of life. **As a Christian you are
able to share in the life of the Father and the Son. All
His heavenly blessings become yours, and you can live
as His friend!**

Jesus has saved you from sin, guilt and shame. He has
saved you from the punishment you deserved. He has saved
you from the devil's grasp and from eternal condemnation in
hell. He has saved you for Himself. He has saved you for His
purposes, to fulfil the plan He has for your life. **He has saved
you to live in fellowship with Him now as His friend.** He
has saved you for an eternal destiny with Him in heaven.

Prayer: *Lord Jesus, thank you that you love me so much that
you came and died for me.*

Four

꙰

Children of God

By faith in Jesus Christ, you have received the right to become a child of God, a son or a daughter in His family. He has given you the Holy Spirit to enable you to live as His child and share in the inheritance Jesus has made possible through His perfect obedience.

Despite your imperfections you can share in His life and receive every blessing that is in Christ, all because of what He has done for you! God's purpose is that you should not only be His child in name, not only receive His blessings, but live as His child, in close relationship with Him!

It is possible to be part of a family and yet not be a close friend with the other family members, even the head of the family. The Lord doesn't want this to be the case with you, or any of His children. It was a wonderful privilege for God to choose you to become part of His family. You are not some distant relative, one among thousands of millions! **He wants you to know Him as your intimate Friend, to live and walk in close relationship with Him.**

Jesus is your Friend, who is with you always and cares about you. He looks to you to be His friend! You can belong to the family of God, yet still live in a formal or distant relationship with Jesus. This is not what He desires.

You can ask yourself: 'Why me?' The answer the Bible gives is simple: **Because He chose you.** He took the initiative, as He did with Saul of Tarsus. Saul became Paul, the apostle, had a very fruitful ministry, and was used by God in many wonderful ways. Before his conversion he was an enemy of Christ and even persecuted Christians. Yet he became a close friend of Jesus. He established churches, saw great numbers of people come to faith in Christ, and he witnessed many healings and miraculous events.

> I thank Christ Jesus our Lord, who has given me strength, that he considered me faithful, appointing me to his service. Even though I was once a blasphemer and a persecutor and a violent man, I was shown mercy because I acted in ignorance and unbelief. The grace of our Lord was poured out on me abundantly, along with the faith and love that are in Christ Jesus.
> (1 Timothy 1:12–14)

Saul of Tarsus seemed a strange choice, but look what he became. The arch-persecutor of the Church became the great apostle to the Gentiles, who wrote nearly half of the New Testament! This transformation was the result of God's mercy, His grace, faith and love, that were poured out on Paul abundantly.

The Lord has shown you His mercy, and is ready to pour out His grace, faith and love on you to enable you to live as His friend.

During the closing period of his life, Paul wrote in prison that he wanted to know Christ! However much you know the Lord, there is still so much more to know! However much you understand of Him there is still so much more to be revealed to you. Paul said:

> I press on to take hold of that for which Christ Jesus took hold of me. Brothers, I do not consider myself yet to

have taken hold of it. But one thing I do: Forgetting what is behind and straining towards what is ahead, I press on towards the goal to win the prize for which God has called me heavenward in Christ Jesus.
(Philippians 3:12–13)

Paul simply longed to know Jesus better. Is this your desire? Do you want to walk more closely with Him, to see Jesus do more in your life and use you more fruitfully?

Jesus told the disciples that He was able to reveal to His friends all that the Father had revealed to Him. Rather than have a superficial relationship with them, He revealed to them the secrets of His Kingdom:

The knowledge of the secrets of the kingdom of heaven has been given to you, but not to them. (Matthew 13:11)

Certain things could only be made known to those who were committed to following Him, and living as His friends.

He wants to reveal to you the secrets of the Kingdom of Heaven, so that you live the life of that Kingdom here on earth! He wants you to follow Him and fulfil the plan He has for your life! No matter what transformation is necessary to bring this about, He is able to work that in you!

Prayer: *Lord Jesus, I want to follow you and live the life of your Kingdom.*

🔊

Five

The Father and the Son

Jesus wants His friends to relate to Him in the same way He related to the Father while He was on earth. His relationship with His Father was the key to His ministry. Only if we understand how He related to the Father, can we understand the way in which He wants us to relate to Him, and how His life can more readily be expressed in our lives.

Jesus continually stated that He did not become man by His own decision; He was sent by the Father for a number of reasons, each of which was important for God's plan of salvation.

Jesus was sent to save the world:

> For God did not send his Son into the world to condemn
> the world, but to save the world through Him.
> (John 3:17)

As we have seen, Jesus came as the Saviour of the world. He is the only one through whom men can become acceptable to God and receive the rich inheritance given to those who belong to the Kingdom of Heaven.

These truths have to be personal for you. Jesus died for **you**. In love He gave His life as a sacrifice to the Father so that you could be forgiven for all the ways you have failed to love Him and others, and to make it possible for you to live in love and obedience now. **As His friend, the Father now sees you cleansed, made righteous and totally**

acceptable to Him. You could not accomplish this by your own efforts or goodness; it is the fruit of His great love for you.

You could only put your faith in what He has done for you. **Then all that is His became yours!** His life becomes your life. He gives you 'the fullness of life', eternal life, God's own life!

What a friend to have! The power of His blood has cleansed you from all past failure. Now you can look forward to the future with a longing to please Him by responding to His love in the way He desires. We love because He has first loved us, and has proved that love by dying for us!

He has broken the power and hold of sin over your life. So now you can live in Him, belong to Him, relate to Him as His friend. **His life is your life; and your life is His, to be lived for His honour and glory!**

Prayer: *Lord Jesus, thank you that you have made me acceptable to God and have given me your life.*

℘

Six

5∂

Sent to Speak the Words of God

> For the one whom God has sent speaks the words of
> God, for God gives the Spirit without limit. (John 3:34)

> For I did not speak of my own accord, but the Father
> who sent me commanded me what to say and how to
> say it. I know that his command leads to eternal life. So
> whatever I say is just what the Father has told me to
> say. (John 12:49–50)

Jesus was the Word through whom God created. That
Word was made flesh and came to live among men. As the
Word of God He spoke the words of God. When we hear
the Son, we hear the Father speaking through the Son!

Even though Jesus is the Word of God, He still could
not choose to say whatever He wanted. Because He had
come to do His Father's will, He had to speak the words His
Father gave him to speak. It is hardly surprising, therefore,
that when Jesus spoke miracles happened: the sick were
healed, the bound were set free, the dead were raised, the
storm abated immediately. All heaven's power and resources supported His words; the supernatural power of
God's Kingdom was released when He spoke.

Paul tells us that **'with the same spirit of faith we
believe and therefore speak'**. The Lord expected creation
to come into being when He spoke. Jesus expected the sick
to be healed when He addressed these needs. As a friend of
Jesus, the Lord wants you to speak into being His purposes

for your life. He wants to see in you the faith that expects things to happen when you speak in His name.

Jesus encouraged His disciples to emulate Him by speaking with faith and authority. He gave them authority over all the power of the evil one. They were to speak to 'mountains', problems and needs in their lives, commanding them to be moved. And they could pray in Jesus's name, expecting to receive whatever they asked!

The same is true for Jesus's friends today. The Spirit will give us the words to speak with authority and power. **And all heaven is poised ready to act in response to our faith. With the same spirit of faith we believe and therefore speak!**

Of course, if you do not obey what Jesus tells you to do, you should not be surprised that you remain stuck with the 'mountains'! When you speak with the spirit of faith you believe in your heart and do not doubt that the problems will be removed! Can God work such a faith in you? Could you speak with such authority and power? Most certainly! Read on!

Prayer: *Lord Jesus, I choose to live by faith in you.*

🔊

Sent to Do the Works of God

> I tell you the truth, the Son can do nothing by himself;
> he can do only the things he sees his Father doing,
> because whatever the Father does the Son also does.
> (John 5:19)

Jesus had a keen sense of timing, and He knew how important it was for Him to obey the direction in which His Father led Him. It is amazing to think that Jesus should live on the earth for thirty years before He started to perform miracles of healing and deliverance. His heart must have yearned to reach out and help the people in need all around Him. Yet He had to wait for the Father's timing, and for the Holy Spirit's anointing before His ministry could begin.

Throughout His ministry He listened to the Father; only then would He know when and how to act. He used various methods of healing, presumably because this is what He was led to do, treating every situation as unique. This is very different from the fixed methods people are prone to use today!

He had to be obedient. Why, when so many sick people lay around the pool of Bethesda, did Jesus only heal one crippled man? Because this is all the Father led Him to do. Even Jesus said that He could do nothing of Himself. So presumably He could not have healed any of the others without a clear leading from His Father. Certainly He would never do anything independently of His Father; He had not come to do His own will, but the will of Him who sent Him.

Apart from Jesus we can do nothing! He wants His friends to walk with Him and be sensitive to the voice of His Spirit so that they know what to do and when to do it. Whenever we obey the Lord we will succeed, for He never wants us to fail. When we act in independence, no matter how good our intentions, we are on our own! It is not surprising if things don't work out as we would like when we ask the Lord to follow us, instead of following Him!

As His friend, you are blessed and He wants to use you to bless others. So listen, be led by Him and obedient to Him, and you will be abundantly fruitful!

Prayer: *Lord Jesus, I want to be sensitive to the voice of your Holy Spirit.*

᷍ᴣᴫ

Sent to Give Life

> For just as the Father raises the dead and gives them
> life, even so the Son gives life to whom he is pleased to
> give it. (John 5:21)

> I have come that they may have life, and have it to the
> full. (John 10:10)

Eternal life is God's life, and only He has the prerogative to impart that life. Jesus came to make it possible for men and women to receive this life now and to live Kingdom life here on earth, as Jesus Himself did. To have eternal life is, therefore, to have the life of Jesus Himself, life in all its fullness.

All those who believe in Him receive that life; God's life now and for all eternity.

The healings and acts of deliverance that Jesus performed were evidences of the power of this life, and were signs that, with Jesus, God was making the life and resources of His heavenly Kingdom available to His children on earth. The same is true of His other miracles, such as the feeding of the multitude, walking on the sea, and turning water into wine.

Jesus demonstrated that eternal life is not an extension of this mortal life, but supernatural life of an altogether different order. It transcends the natural and is infinitely more powerful.

This is the life and power God wants to see evidenced in

your life as His disciple and friend. He also wants His character to be reflected in you. Because God is love, to have fullness of life is to have love in all its fullness. Because He is merciful, as a child of His Kingdom you are also to be merciful. Because He is gracious, as His friend you are to be full of grace.

All His qualities are made available to you through the impartation of His life, so that you may reflect those qualities in your life. You cannot express what you have not first received!

Paul says: 'You have been given fullness in Christ Jesus' (Colossians 2:10). **He wants you to learn to exercise the power and authority that is given you through having that life, but also to see its characteristics reflected increasingly in you.**

Perhaps you do not realize fully what power is already yours as a believer in Jesus Christ. The closer you walk with Jesus as His friend, the more these things will become a reality in your experience. His love, life and power will flow out of your life more freely! You need to understand how this can happen in reality instead of being only a grand idea!

Prayer: *Lord Jesus, I want to see your love, life and power*
expressed in my life.

꒱

Sent to Do the Will of God

> For I have come down from heaven not to do my will,
> but to do the will of him who sent me. (John 6:38)

> The one who sent me is with me; he has not left me
> alone, for I always do what pleases him. (John 8:29)

> Do not believe me unless I do what the Father does.
> (John 10:37)

Jesus had not been sent to fulfil His own purpose, but His Father's will. He not only lived in a relationship of love and unity with His Father, but also in submission to Him. He never acted independently of the Father. It is an amazing statement to suggest that people should not believe Him unless He did what the Father did! How many other preachers would dare say such a thing?

Jesus could preach obedience to His Father's will because He was always obedient Himself! He lived with this tension: On the one hand He could say, 'The Father and I are One'; on the other, 'The Father is greater than I.'

As His friends we live with a similar tension. By His mercy and grace we are born again. God has taken hold of us and placed us in Christ. Now we live in Him and His life is in us. We are one with Him, but He is so much greater than we are.

Therefore it is for every believer to live in submission to Jesus as Lord and Master. All Christians have to decide that Jesus is the King of their lives and has every right to reign over them. This is what it means to belong to His Kingdom!

If He is your Lord and King, then it is His will and purpose that needs to prevail in your life. He is to exercise His authority over you; then you will be able to exercise authority in His name. By submitting to His authority, you can exercise His authority!

We do not allow Him to be Lord when we disobey Him! Disobedience is rebellion against His authority, and renders us incapable of using the authority He makes available to us.

In obedience Jesus came. In obedience He lived. In obedience He went to the cross. And now He reigns in glory as the reward for that obedience. He could pray: 'I have brought you glory on earth by completing the work you gave me to do' (John 17:4). He cried triumphantly on the cross 'It is finished', or 'It is accomplished', or 'It is done'. He had completed the work of salvation by making His life a sacrifice on our behalf.

As His friend, Jesus calls you to walk with Him in obedience to the Father, and so complete the work He has for you to do. You are a 'fellow worker' with Christ. You have work to do; not your own work, but the work He assigns you.

However, you do not set about this work merely as a servant, although it is a great privilege to serve the King of Kings. You fulfil this work as His friend, content to obey Him because of who He is: your greatest and closest friend, who loves you so much that He has died for you and given you His own life! **To fulfil His purposes you will need to live in the good of the power He gives you and the authority He makes available to you.**

Prayer: *Lord Jesus, I submit to your will for my life.*

Ten

🔊

Sent to Reveal the Father

I am not here on my own, but he who sent me is true.
(John 7:28)

I know him because I am from him and he sent me.
(John 7:29)

He who sent me is reliable, and what I have heard from
him I tell the world. (John 8:26)

I and the Father are one. (John 10:30)

Jesus came to make friends! And He has chosen those who
are to be His friends. To them He makes known everything
He has learned from the Father. He desires to hold nothing
back from them!

Because it was His purpose to reveal the Father, Jesus
had to be obedient to Him. God cannot be revealed
through disobedience, nor any other form of sin! Whatever
Jesus did had to reveal God's heart and will. So He maintained a close fellowship with His Father in prayer, and was
sensitive to His Father's voice.

There are those who desire more of God's power, but
without the relationship necessary for a proper use of that
power. They pray for more anointing, but don't necessarily
want to know Jesus better, or be obedient to Him.

Because of our self-love, we don't like the idea of obedience. We would prefer to have all the blessings God offers
without any cost to ourselves. We would like Him to give

us whatever we ask for, irrespective of the way we live.

Every blessing, every gift, every work of God in our lives is a work of His grace. **We deserve nothing; He has chosen to give us everything**. Through God's mercy we receive the very opposite of what we deserve!

Yet Jesus came to fulfil God's law, not destroy it. He came to make obedience possible for us through the enabling of God's Spirit. **We are to love Him with all our heart, mind, soul and strength. We are to love our neighbours as ourselves. And Jesus added the new commandment: to love one another as He has loved us.**

The Father still expects obedience. Because He has given us new life and placed His Spirit within us to make obedience possible, we have far less excuse for disobedience than was the case under the law for:

> Through Christ Jesus the law of the Spirit of life set me free from the law of sin and death. For what the law was powerless to do in that it was weakened by the sinful nature, God did by sending his own Son in the likeness of sinful man to be a sin offering. And so he condemned sin in sinful man, in order that the righteous requirements of the law might be fully met in us, who do not live according to the sinful nature but according to the Spirit. (Romans 8:2–4)

You have been set free from the law of sin and death. The Spirit of life now lives in you. The righteous requirements of the law can be fully met in you, by His grace. Jesus expects you to be obedient. 'You are my friends if you do what I command.'

Prayer: *Lord Jesus, I want to be full of love for you.*

Sent For Judgement

For judgement I have come into the world, so that the blind will see and those who see will become blind. (John 9:39)

And he has given him authority to judge because He is the Son of Man. (John 5:27)

The Father had entrusted all judgement to Jesus. However, He came not to judge but to save people from the judgement they deserved. At the same time He also makes it clear that people were judged by their response to Him. Those who believed in Him were spared the condemnation they deserved, for there is no condemnation for those who belong to Christ Jesus.

On the other hand, those who rejected Jesus and refused to put their trust in Him, condemned themselves by their unbelief. Even though Jesus's intention was to save through the mercy God extended to those who turned to Him, He spoke also of the dire consequences of rejecting Him and the Gospel He proclaimed. To reject the truth is to reject the opportunity to receive eternal life!

The reason for this is simple. God's judgement on sin has not changed. Any sin renders the sinner worthy of death.

We are made worthy, not through anything we have done, but through the worthiness of Christ. Now we are accepted 'in the beloved' and He wants us to fulfil His purposes by obediently walking in His way, doing what He asks of us and having fruitful lives that will give Him glory.

Faith in Jesus turns us from sinners into saints. A saint is one God has called and set apart to be His child, one who is made holy in His sight through being cleansed by the blood of Jesus!

Saints are to live as saints, not sinners! Every Christian will have to give account personally to the Father for the way in which he or she has lived the new life.

Salvation is a gift from God, a work of His grace. Through that gift you have an assurance of your place in heaven. However, Jesus makes it clear that every believer will be rewarded for what he or she has done. Not all will have the same reward in heaven.

The way we live the new life, and the fruit produced in our lives, will be of great significance as far as our eternal status in heaven is concerned. This is a truth many don't want to face. They want to rejoice that they are saved by the grace of God, without facing the responsibilities involved in living the new life!

The Lord has shown us His great mercy in forgiving us all our sins and making us completely acceptable before Him in Christ. Now we are to live in Christ. And He will live His life out in each one of us. We are to abide in Christ and He in us.

Jesus warns not only of the eternal perils of rejecting Him and the salvation He offers. He warns also, through many of the parables He taught, of the consequences of a disobedient life – and the rewards for obedience.

This is the choice before every believer: obedience or disobedience. It is a misuse of God's grace to suggest that it doesn't matter how we live as Christians, because we are assured of His forgiveness as soon as we repent. **The Lord** has not saved us for disobedience and a life of continual sin, but for obedience to Him so that His purposes may be fulfilled.

Jesus taught us to pray: 'May your will be done on earth as it is in heaven.' To pray these words with integrity, the believer's desire needs to be: 'May your will be done in my life, as it is in heaven.' He wants to please the Lord He loves!

His friends obey His commands! Not out of a fear of the consequences of disobedience, but out of love for Him!

Prayer: *Lord Jesus, I want to obey you.*

 ♪

Twelve

🔖

Sent to Live in Dependence
on the Father

By myself I can do nothing. (John 5:30)

I love the Father and I do exactly what the Father has
commanded me. (John 14:31)

It is astonishing that the Son of God confessed that He
could do nothing by Himself! To Jesus it was unthinkable
that He should do anything independently of His Father.
That would be sin on His part. He was sent to live in obedience and therefore in dependence upon His Father, not
in independence!

Jesus, therefore, lived by faith. He is the Author and Perfecter of our faith because He lived by faith Himself. To live
in complete dependence on the Father is the essence of a
life of faith!

**Just as faith was a way of life for Jesus, so it is to be
for us!** By faith in Him we receive eternal life. Those who
came to Him in faith were healed. He taught the disciples
to pray with faith, telling them that they would receive
whatever they asked in prayer if they believed. If they
spoke to 'mountains' with faith, their problems would be
removed. **All things would become possible for them if
they believed.** They would lay hands on the sick and they
would recover. They could cast out demons and even raise
the dead!

Jesus was frustrated when His disciples failed to act with

28

faith. He told them they were slow to believe. He called His disciples 'a faithless and perverse generation'. He rebuked them for not believing that He would rise from the dead.

Peter began to walk on water, but then his faith wavered and he began to sink. When he cried out for Jesus to save him, He did so but asked, 'Why did you doubt, O man of little faith?'

In Scripture we are told that without faith it is impossible to please God, and all that is not of faith is sin! The only way to fulfil God's purposes is through faith in Him. This is why Paul says that the only thing that matters is faith being expressed in love. And this is a precise description of Jesus's own ministry. This is the way He lived, by faith being expressed in love!

The life of faith is a life of obedience. Faith is not trying to make God do what you want; it is living in obedience to His Word, believing His promises. When we respond to God's initiatives we are always successful. When we take the initiative away from Him, we begin to act in presumption not faith.

When we do what He tells us to do, He does what He promises to do. As a friend of Jesus, you are called to a life of faith, to live dependent on the Father, knowing He will never fail you!

Prayer: *Lord Jesus, I choose to depend on you, not myself.*

ॐ

Sent to Give His Life

> The reason my Father loves me is that I lay down my
> life – only to take it up again. No one takes it from me,
> but I lay it down of my own accord. I have authority
> to lay it down and authority to take it up again. This
> command I received from my Father. (John 10:17–18)

> My heart is troubled, and what shall I say? 'Father, save
> me from this hour'? No, it was for this very reason that
> I came to this hour. (John 12:27)

This is another surprising statement that Jesus made, for it
seems to suggest that the Father's love for Him was dependent in some way on His obedience. One act of disobedience or independence would have had the same effect on
their relationship as Adam's disobedience in the Garden of
Eden. Jesus had been sent to repair the damage done by
Adam's sin, not to repeat it!

It was only by becoming man, living a life of perfect
obedience and submission, and then offering His perfect
life on the cross as a sacrifice, that the sin of Adam could be
undone. In living like this Jesus demonstrated His love
both for His Father and for us.

It is impossible for us to understand the greatness of
God's love for us, that He should deliberately send His only
Son to take upon Himself the judgement and punishment
we deserve for our sins, our disobedience and even rebellion against God's sovereign purpose and will! Jesus had to

suffer the agony of the Garden of Gethsemane to undo the sin of the Garden of Eden. Then He had to endure the pain and rejection of the cross for our healing and eternal acceptance by God! What love!

The whole of our lives is a response to this love. **We love because He first loved us!**

If obedience cost Jesus the laying down of His life, will it involve anything less for us? He laid down His life for us and so we will be required to lay down our lives for one another.

This is the cross you are willingly to take up day by day in order to follow Jesus. He will not force such a cross upon you; it has to be the fruit of your love for Him, coming from your desire to please Him.

Love requires sacrifice, or it is unreal. When two people 'fall in love', they are prepared to make all kinds of sacrifices for one another. If we love the Lord, then we love His people also and will want to show His love to them in practical ways, even though at times this will be both inconvenient and costly. Jesus said:

> If you refuse to take up your cross and follow me, you are not worthy of being mine. If you cling to your life, you will lose it; but if you give it up for me, you will find it. (Matthew 10:38–39; NLT)

You have a cross to carry; but not Jesus's cross. You could never make your life a sinless sacrifice as He did. Neither is this a cross of suffering or sickness that is laid upon you. **Your cross is what you undertake willingly for the Lord and His Kingdom, making your body a living sacrifice, allowing Him to use you to serve Him and love others in the way He asks of you.**

Your cross will seem a burden to you unless you take it up willingly, out of love for Jesus. Even He could only endure His cross because of His loving obedience to the Father, and His love for all of us for whom He gave His life. To Him be praise for evermore!

Love is only inconvenient to our own plans and costly to our flesh! The failure to love others, or to give the Lord the time needed in prayer to build a strong relationship with Him, demonstrates a lack of love on our part. All disobedience is a preferring of 'self' to God, despite all He has done for us in love.

The greater your thankfulness to Jesus for His love for you, the more willing you will be to express His love for others!

Prayer: *Lord Jesus, I choose to take up my cross daily to follow you.*

🔾

Fourteen

৯৯

Sent to Bring Glory to the Father

Now is the Son of Man glorified and God is glorified in
him. If God is glorified in him, God will glorify the
Son in himself, and will glorify him at once.
(John 13:31–32)

In everything Jesus wanted to bring glory to His Father; by
obeying His will, by speaking the words He was given to
speak, by doing the things He saw His Father doing, by
laying His life down for His friends! Everything He did was
to reveal and glorify His Father; He never sought His own
glory – until He was facing the reality of the cross. He
looked beyond that event to the glory that was set before
Him in heaven, to being restored to the place that was
rightfully His. This restoration would be the eternal reward
for His obedience and sacrifice.

It was necessary for Jesus to go to the cross of His own
free will. The Father did not force Him to be crucified or to
obey Him in any other respect. As a result of His obedience, Jesus bore much fruit. One seed had to fall into the
ground and die; but from that one seed a vast multitude
has been born into God's Kingdom.

This is the principle by which the Lord asks us to live as
His friends. If we seek to hold on to our lives we will lose
them, Jesus warns. But if we lose them for His sake and for
the Gospel, then we shall find them.

What was true for Paul is true also for you:

I have been crucified with Christ and I no longer live, but Christ lives in me. The life I now live in the body, I live by faith in the Son of God, who loved me and gave himself for me. (Galatians 2:20)

When Jesus went to the cross, He took not only your sin – He took you the sinner. When He died, you died; all mankind died!

When He arose from the dead, all those who were to put their faith in Him rose with Him. So, as a believer, you now share in the risen life of Jesus Christ. Paul says:

You died, and your life is now hidden with Christ in God. When Christ, who is your life, appears, then you also will appear with him in glory. (Colossians 3:3–4)

Meanwhile you are called to live this new life:

Or don't you know that all of us who were baptized into Christ Jesus were baptized into His death? We were therefore buried with him through baptism into death in order that, just as Christ was raised from the dead through the glory of the Father, we too may live a new life. (Romans 6:3–4)

Because you have died with Christ and have been raised to a new life in Him, you are to offer yourself as a slave not to sin, but to 'obedience, which leads to righteousness' (Romans 6:16).

Righteousness is not only being in a right position before God; it is **doing** what is right in His sight. Jesus was righteous by nature; He therefore did the works of righteousness.

Through taking us to the cross, He has made us

righteous, so that now we may do the works of righteousness.

You look forward to living and rejoicing with Him in glory. Meanwhile there is work to be done: the good things Jesus has prepared for you as His friend! The fruit that will bring glory to the Father!

Prayer: *Lord Jesus, thank you that I died with you and can now live a new life.*

৯৯

Sent with Authority

For you granted him authority over all people that he
might give eternal life to all those you have given him.
(John 17:2)

Jesus always acted with authority, even His opponents recognized that. Nobody taught with such authority, or exer-
cised such power over the demonic, sickness and even
death.

The Roman centurion was commended by Jesus for his
faith because he recognized that authority lay behind the
power He demonstrated. He saw also that **the secret of
having authority is to be submissive to the authority
over you.** As a soldier, the centurion had to be submissive
to his superior officers if he was to be allowed to exercise
authority over those under him.

The same principle applied to Jesus. **By being obedient
and submissive to His Father, Jesus could exercise the
Father's authority in all the ways demonstrated in His
ministry.**

Jesus would not allow anything to disrupt His relationship of perfect unity with His Father. Without perfect submission to the Father's authority, there would be no
salvation. The eternal destiny of millions was at stake and
assured through the obedience of one Man!

Through His submission to the Father's authority, Jesus
could exercise the authority to give eternal life to all who

were given Him by the Father to be His friends! The Father entrusts certain people to Him so that Jesus can impart eternal life to them. He will present these same people back to the Father perfect and without blemish. Because you belong to Him you are one of those people!

Jesus has given you that life and you now can live that life in dependence on Him. As you do this, you will be able to exercise the spiritual authority He has given you! No one can prevent you from being obedient to Him! It is for you to choose to submit yourself to His authority, to do His will and fulfil His purposes for your life. The greater your submission to Him, the more you will be able to exercise His authority.

Prayer: *Lord Jesus, thank you for the spiritual authority you have given me.*

𝔖𝔸

Sixteen

Friends Are in Christ

If you are a believer in Jesus, He has called you to be His disciple, to follow Him and be His friend. You are a believer, follower, disciple, friend of Jesus and called to be one with Him! Jesus told the disciples: 'Remain in me and I will remain in you.'

You can only remain where you have been put by God the Father: in Christ Jesus. As you continue to live in Him, so He will continue to live in you. How can you live in Him? How can you know Him better and experience the power of His love in your life? How can He work in your heart so that you are able to relate with other believers in a deeper bond of love than you have known in the past?

> I am the bread of life. He who comes to me will never go hungry, and he who believes in me will never go thirsty. (John 6:35)

> All that the Father gives me will come to me, and whoever comes to me I will never drive away. (John 6:37)

> No one can come to me unless the Father who sent me draws him, and I will raise him up at the last day. (John 6:44)

> Everyone who listens to the Father and learns from him comes to me. (John 6:45)

You 'came to Jesus' when you first gave Him your life. You need to keep coming to Him, turning to Him, looking to Him, relying on Him! This is to be a continual process!

The Father wanted you to be a friend of Jesus. He specifically chose to place you in Christ. Just as Jesus lived 'in the Father' and the Father 'in Him', so you are to live in Christ Jesus, and He in you. The Lord does not want you to see yourself as being independent of Jesus, but in Him, sharing His life.

Because you are in Christ, His life has become your life. Everything He has becomes your inheritance. God has blessed you in Christ with every spiritual blessing in heavenly places!

Because you live in Him, He does not want you to go hungry; rather He is ready to feed you with the living bread of His Word. Jesus said:

> Man does not live on bread alone, but on every word
> that comes from the mouth of God. (Matthew 4:4)

Jesus's words are your daily spiritual food. As you feed on His words, He continues to impart His Spirit and life to you. Every day you can 'sit at His feet' and allow Him to teach you, to reveal to you the nature of all the blessings you have in Christ! You can learn how He is able to express His life in and through you.

Jesus remained in the Father by being obedient to Him; you will remain in Christ by being obedient to Him, by allowing His words to live in you! Obedience enables you to live in Christ; disobedience is a denial of your privilege of being in Him! All sin distances you from Jesus. He is still with you, but at a distance! The sin opens a gap between you and the Lord. That gap is closed when you are forgiven, making it possible for you to continue to live in Him.

However, Jesus does not want you to jump in and out of Him, obeying Him one moment, choosing to please yourself the next. He wants to see consistent obedience in your life. And this obedience will be the fruit of your love for Him.

Come to Him daily in prayer, learning to pour your heart out to Him and listen to what He has to say to you. Learn to turn to Him at any moment of the day, knowing He is always with you and ready to help you.

Jesus will never drive you away when you come to Him. He will never tire of you being His friend. Even when you have ignored His words, or deliberately disobeyed what He has said, He wants to restore you as quickly as possible so that you will walk again in His ways and bear fruit that will glorify the Father in your life.

And Jesus will bring you to the fulfilment of God's call: He will raise you up on the last day. Then you will be able to receive the reward for your obedience. You will enjoy eternal friendship with your Lord, your Saviour and King.

Nobody can understand such wonderful love that moves the Father to call sinners to Himself, forgive them and place them in His Son so they can one day be presented back to Him perfect and spotless, able to inherit the eternal blessings of heaven!

For my Father's will is that everyone who looks to the Son and believes in him shall have eternal life, and I will raise him up at the last day. (John 6:40)

You have responded to His call, and He will work His purpose out in you!

We have already seen that faith is the response we make to God's initiative in extending His grace and mercy to us. He gives us the very opposite of what we deserve. Instead of condemnation, judgement, death and eternal separation from God, He has given us forgiveness, peace, reconciliation and a rich inheritance.

Prayer: *Lord Jesus, thank you that I live in you, and you live in me.*

Friends Pray and Act in Faith

We are to do the works of faith because we live in a faith relationship with Jesus. The initial act of faith in response to hearing the Gospel puts us into this wonderful relationship with Jesus Christ. Paul wrote:

> And you also were included in Christ when you heard the word of truth, the gospel of your salvation. Having believed, you were marked in him with a seal, the promised Holy Spirit, who is a deposit guaranteeing our inheritance until the redemption of those who are God's possession – to the praise of his glory.
> (Ephesians 1:13–14)

You could not live in Christ until you believed in Him. You now continue to live in Him through faith in His Word. Christ's life has become your life. His righteousness is your righteousness; His holiness is your holiness; His peace your peace; His joy your joy; His inheritance your inheritance. **You are completely identified with Him.** You need to believe this, instead of looking back and thinking you are still the person you used to be before your new birth.

Once you lived in darkness; now you are a child of light. Once you had no claim upon God; now you live in Him and He in you. Once you had no inheritance; now you have a rich inheritance, for all the riches and resources of heaven are yours. He has blessed you in Christ with every spiritual blessing in heavenly places.

The Lord never wants you to lose sight of all He has done for you, and the rich inheritance you have in Christ. Rather, He wants you to lay hold of all that He has made yours in Jesus. Faith reaches up to heaven to take hold of that which the Lord says in His Word belongs to you. Faith believes that He will be faithful in giving whatever He has promised.

It is not for the believer to say how He is to give, or when; but to trust in His promises. **The believer is to believe!** And when he or she does so, God acts. We **must** believe that He rewards those who earnestly seek Him.

When Jesus says, 'Ask, and you will receive', the word is in the continual present tense and means: 'Go on asking', 'Continue to ask'. When you pray with faith, you are determined to receive the answers you need!

Jesus's friends are not put off by events or circumstances, for faith in Jesus enables Him to change situations through His supernatural power, often in dramatic, unexpected ways.

When you pray with faith, you are not prepared to accept any answer, but only the right one! The Lord likes boldness and determination of faith, reaching out to Him for the fulfilment of His promises! Jesus never taught His disciples to expect the answer, 'No'!

Paul suffered for the sake of the Gospel, but never allowed adverse circumstances to distract him from God's purposes. In the most dire situations Paul always looked for the positive. Even when he was in prison he could write to others and tell them to rejoice in the Lord always!

This is the nature of a true and living faith. It turns you from a victim to a victor. The Lord wants to change your attitudes so that you think with the mind of Christ.

This means your thoughts will be in line with the revelation of truth God gives us in His Word.

The closer you walk with Jesus, the easier it is to hear His voice and receive from Him the words of faith you need. The more you hear Him, the more you will trust Him. **If you trust Him, you will not be overcome by events. Rather, with His grace to enable you, you will overcome.** One thing Jesus cannot do is to fail! So whenever you trust Him, you will not fail either!

However, you cannot think in one way when you pray, and in another for the rest of the time. Faith is a relationship with Jesus, a walk with Him, trusting Him all the time, not only when you pray. Your flesh life, your natural self, tends to be negative; the Spirit of God is positive. He reminds you of what the Lord says in His Word.

Faith comes from hearing the Word of God spoken to your heart by the Spirit. The more you hear Him, the more you will trust Him. **To live as His friend is to know that He is completely trustworthy, that He will always be with you as He has promised, and that He will never leave you nor forsake you. He is for you and wants to help you in every situation.**

Don't say to yourself that you are unable to hear the Lord! You only have to open your Bible and He will speak to you. It is good to do this before you pray, for then your thinking will tend to be more in line with God's thinking. **You will be more aware of His greatness and the wonderful promises He gives to those who believe in Him!**

Prayer: *Lord Jesus, thank you for being with me always and enabling me to overcome.*

Eighteen

Friends Follow Jesus

He calls his own sheep by name and leads them out.
When he has brought all his own, he goes on ahead of
them, and his sheep follow him because they know his
voice. (John 10:3–4)

My sheep listen to my voice; I know them and they follow me. (John 10:27)

Whoever serves me must follow me; and where I am,
my servant also will be. (John 12:26)

Jesus knows personally each one who belongs to Him. You
might feel that you need to know Him much better than
you do at present. This is understandable. However, Jesus
already knows you perfectly. He knows you by name. He
speaks to you every day through His Holy Spirit living
within you. He has a plan and purpose for your life, which
is part of the universal plan He is working out in history.
And one day He will present you spotless and without fault
to the Father so that you can live and reign with Him for all
eternity!

Not only did Jesus take the initiative in calling you into
His Kingdom; He wants to maintain that initiative. He is
the good Shepherd. He leads His sheep. **So it is not for
you to tell the Shepherd what to do; neither are you to
get ahead of the Shepherd. You follow His lead.**

This is for your own good. He will lead you beside still
waters and into rich pastures. He will lead you through the

fire so that you will not be burned and through the waters so that you will not be drowned.

> Do not be afraid, for I have ransomed you. I have called you, you are mine. When you go through deep waters and great trouble, I will be with you. When you go through rivers of difficulty, you will not drown! When you walk through the fire of oppression, you will not be burned up; the flames will not consume you. For I am the Lord, your God, the Holy One of Israel, your Saviour. (Isaiah 43:1–3; NLT)

To live with Jesus is to live in His security. This is why Jesus was dismayed at the lack of faith His disciples showed when they were with Him in the boat, afraid that they would drown in the storm. They should have realized their security lay in the fact that they were with Him. If He said they were going to the other side of the lake, that is exactly what would happen, and nothing would be able to prevent this!

Never listen to your fears; listen to your faith! When you look at the circumstances or your own weakness and lack of ability, you will be tempted to fear. But Jesus's answer to fear was to tell His disciples not to fear – for He was with them! They did not need ministry or prayer for their fears; they needed to trust Him!

How can you know that Jesus is with you and still be afraid? He is so much bigger than any situation or problem. Even if your natural reaction is to fear, your faith will enable you to overcome the fear. If you listen to your fears you will be paralysed into inactivity.

> Even though I walk through the valley of the shadow of death [*lit.* through the darkest valley], I will fear no evil,

for you are with me; your rod and staff they comfort me.
(Psalm 23:4)

Jesus tells us not to worry about what to eat or drink, what
to wear, or about tomorrow's events.

Worry never accomplishes anything.

Who of you by worrying can add a single hour to his
life? (Matthew 6:27)

In His sovereign oversight of our lives the Lord knows that
each day has enough troubles of its own. He has given us
the grace to trust Him so that we will not be overcome by
today's events. However, **He does not give you grace for
tomorrow until tomorrow! So if you start worrying
about tomorrow you place yourself outside His plan
and purpose for today!**

Let Jesus be a Friend to you, one in whom you can confide and on whom you can depend. Walk day by day with
Jesus as your Friend and you will discover the same truth
as He revealed to Paul:

My grace is sufficient for you, for my power is made perfect in weakness. (2 Corinthians 12:9)

Let awareness of your weakness encourage you to put your
confidence in Jesus. He will not fail you. He is your good
Shepherd. As you trust in Him you will lack nothing!

Prayer: *Lord Jesus, thank you that I do not need to fear
anything because you are with me.*

Nineteen

༈

Friends Possess God's Life

I have come that they may have life, and have it to the full. (John 10:10)

By faith we are to lay hold of our inheritance, so we can live in the good of all that God has done for us and given us in Christ. We are to live in the fullness of His life **NOW**. This is why He came and why He has called us to be His friends: to impart to us the fullness of life **NOW**; to enjoy that life **NOW**; to live in the good of that life **NOW**.

Unbelief is the greatest problem for most Christians. God not only promises what He will do; He reveals what He has done. The tenses of verbs in the Bible are very important. They tell us what God has done, what He is doing now and what He promises to do in the future. If He says He has done something already, then He has done it!

Sometimes Christians ask God to do what He has done already! Instead, they need to live in the revelation that what God says is theirs, is indeed theirs!

It will take you the whole of your lifetime to live in the good of what the Lord did for you when you received your new birth. The following list includes some of the things God says are part of the new life He has given you in Christ.

The old has gone and the new has come!
You are a new creation.

He has given you a new heart and has put His Spirit
  within you.

He has forgiven all your sins.

You are now accepted by God 'in the beloved'.

You have been placed 'in Christ Jesus'.

He is your righteousness – God regards you as
  righteous because you are in Christ.

He is your holiness – God regards you as holy and
 ' perfect in Christ.

He has redeemed you; He has paid the price for you so
  that you belong eternally to the Father.

There is no condemnation for you because you are in
  Christ Jesus.

You have fullness of life in Him.

Through His wounds He has healed you.

You are now a child of God.

You are a co-heir with Christ.

You now belong to His covenant of grace.

He has blessed you in Christ with every spiritual
  blessing in heavenly places.

The promises of both the New and the Old Testaments
  are yours.

He has given you victory through Christ Jesus.

It is for freedom Christ has set you free.

You lack no spiritual gift.

He has enriched you in every way.

You are now a child of light and do not need to walk
  in darkness any longer.

He has broken the power of sin in your life, for you
  are set free from the law of sin and death.

Now the Spirit of life operates in you.

You have received the power that raised Jesus from

**the dead, because you have been filled with the Holy Spirit.
And the Holy Spirit is the guarantee of your inheritance that is to come.**

And these are only some of the blessings that are yours in Christ! You don't need to ask the Lord to give you what He has already given! Use your faith to thank the Lord that you have what He says you have, that He has done what He says He has done.

The enemy wants you to concentrate on yourself, your feelings, your dilemmas and problems, and doubt that all these things could truly be yours. Don't be fooled by him. He is the thief who wants to steal, kill and destroy. He cannot take from you what Jesus has chosen to give you. But if he can deceive you into believing that you do not have what God says you do have, then you will not live in the good of your inheritance!

Therefore you are to stand against the enemy; he is a liar and the deceiver of the brethren.

Jesus, on the other hand, is the truth. And His words are words of truth. Even though heaven and earth pass away, His words will never pass away.

See yourself in Christ as God sees you! Believe you have all that He says you have and can do all He says you can do!

Prayer: *Lord Jesus, thank you that all these truths are truths
about me.*

ॐ

Twenty

Friends Receive the Holy Spirit

> Whoever believes in me, as the Scripture has said, streams of living water will flow from within him. By this he meant the Spirit, whom those who believed in him were later to receive. (John 7:38–39)

> And I will ask the Father, and he will give you another Counsellor to be with you forever – the Spirit of truth. (John 14:16–17)

> But the Counsellor, the Holy Spirit, whom the Father will send in my name, will teach you all things and will remind you of everything I have said to you. (John 14:26)

> When he, the Spirit of truth, comes, he will guide you into all the truth. He will not speak on his own; he will speak only what he hears, and he will tell you what is yet to come. (John 16:13)

The Holy Spirit is God. He is promised to all those who believe in Jesus. All believers are to be baptized with the Holy Spirit and live 'submerged' in the Spirit so they over-flow with the life, love and power of the Spirit! 'You anoint my head with oil; my cup overflows' (Psalm 23:5).

When speaking of the Holy Spirit, Jesus says that streams of living water are to flow out of believers. He is concerned not only with what the Christian receives, but also with what flows out of his or her life.

Your body is a temple of the Holy Spirit, of God's

presence. It is the task of the Holy Spirit to reproduce Jesus's character in you, to express His life through you, and enable you to do the same things as Jesus did!

You cannot live the Christian life in your own strength. Jesus recognized that your flesh life, your self life, was worth nothing and could not please God. It was for this reason that you were crucified with Him. Now you have a new life, Christ in you, the hope of glory.

It is possible for a person to say he has given his heart to the Lord and Jesus has come to live in his heart. This sounds very spiritual, but does not mean that he necessarily does anything or produces fruit to glorify the Father.

You are to present **your body** as a living sacrifice, holy and acceptable to God. This is the spiritual worship that God requires. Why? **Because He makes your *body* a temple of His Spirit so that He can use your *body* to express His character and life, to express His love by serving and caring for others.**

There is little point in giving Him your heart unless you are prepared to give Him your body also! Friends of Jesus give Him their bodies, because they know it is not possible to obey Him otherwise! The Lord for the body, and the body for the Lord!

It is futile to try to create a life of your own, apart from Christ. You have a new identity because you have a new life. Now that God lives in you by the person, life and power of the Holy Spirit, He will give life and strength to your mortal body!

He will not live your life *for* you; but He will live His life *in* you. Your life is now to be lived in continual co-operation with the Holy Spirit. Jesus tells us that the Holy Spirit will remind us of all that Jesus has said and done on our behalf. He does not want us to try to do for ourselves what He has already done for us!

He has laid down His life for His friends so that now His Spirit can live in us to guide us into all the truth, and to enable our lives to be a demonstration of the truth.

The Holy Spirit is God's Counsellor within you. He is the voice of God within you. He is ready to speak to you all day long, whether you listen or not! He does not speak from His own initiative, but He speaks only what He hears. In other words, He gives you God's instructions from heaven so that you can fulfil the Lord's plan and purpose. He is concerned about every detail of your life, and wants to teach you how to live in co-operation with God!

He not only tells you what God wants you to do; He is the one who enables you to do it.

Jesus gives His Holy Spirit to His friends to enable them to live as His friends, to enable obedience to His commands. **No matter what personal weaknesses and inadequacies you have, you are able to do whatever God asks of you. You can hear the voice of God and do the will of God through the activity of the Holy Spirit within you.**

Prayer: *Lord Jesus, thank you that my body is a temple of your Holy Spirit.*

৯৯

Twenty-One

5/2

Friends Are Set Free

If you hold to my teaching, you are really my disciples.
Then you will know the truth, and the truth will set
you free. (John 8:31–32)

So if the Son sets you free, you will be free indeed
(John 8:36)

Everybody needs to be free, and Jesus died to set us free!
By the cross we are set free from guilt, from sin, from legal-
istic religion, from sickness, from everything that curses us.
We are even set free from ourselves!

To know that you are crucified with Christ is the secret
to knowing that the person you once were is dead and
buried. Now your life lies hidden with Christ in God! You
no longer live for yourself, but for Him who gave His life
for you. You are set free from your past to follow Christ and
to fulfil whatever purpose He has for you.

You have been set free to live as a friend of Jesus.
There is nothing to hinder you from doing this, if this is
your desire. You become your own hindrance if you choose
your ways instead of His. There are no excuses for disobedience to the Lord. You disobey only because you want to
do so, not because you are unable to obey Him!

Some look at themselves and imagine they are not free,
that their imperfections and inadequacies will inevitably
cause them to fail the Lord. Paul asserts that 'it is for
freedom Christ has set us free' (Galatians 5:1). He has
already done everything to enable you to live in freedom.

'You, my brothers, were called to be free' (Galatians 5:13).

Jesus **has** set you free. Believe Him and thank Him, although often your feelings, experiences and memories will tempt you to think you are not free! How can you say you are free if you don't feel free?

On the cross Jesus 'was wounded and crushed for our sins. He was beaten that we might have peace. He was whipped, and we were healed! ... He was oppressed and treated badly. It was the Lord's good plan to crush him and fill him with grief' (Isaiah 53:5, 7, 10; NLT). He identified completely with every human need to deliver people from their needs. **No matter what your problems, past or present, Jesus dealt with all of them on the cross.**

Jesus told the disciples that knowing the truth was the way to be set free. It is not through methods of ministry or counselling techniques that you will live in freedom, but through knowing and believing the truth of His Word! You will never live in freedom by looking at yourself, but only by looking at Jesus and believing what He has done for you!

The truth can only set you free when you 'know' it. To know the truth is to believe it, which means that you not only accept it as true, but you apply it to your life.

When circumstances seem to contradict the Word, it is the circumstances that need to change, not the Word!

When your feelings or opinion of yourself contradict the revelation of God's Word, choose to believe what the Word says, not your feelings!

You will need to speak the truth about your new life in Christ to yourself, to your circumstances, to the enemy when he attacks. If Jesus has already carried your burdens, you do not need to carry them too! So don't think and speak of yourself as one who is burdened, bound, oppressed or rejected.

Unbelief is a form of pride, thinking we know better than the revelation of truth God has given us, and exalting our own minds above the mind of Christ! Placing our thoughts higher than His thoughts, when in reality His thoughts are so much higher than our own! Unbelief is choosing to believe what you think, rather than what He says.

It sometimes seems unreal at first to say that you are free, healed, forgiven, when you do not feel like that. Your feelings are not the ultimate truth.

Truth is a person: Jesus. To be a friend of Jesus is to be a friend of the Truth. To walk with Him is to live with the Truth. To live with Him is to live with the Truth. To live in Him is to live in the Truth! Your feelings, experiences, circumstances will change – the truth never will!

The truth will not set you free while the words of truth remain in the Bible; they need to be established in your heart! And the Holy Spirit is given you to enable that. He will guide you into all the truth.

You are free to pray as much as you want, to worship whenever you choose, to love those God places before you. You are free to believe what God's Word says, or what you feel! You make the choices. You can give as much of your heart and life to Jesus as you want. You are free to love Him with all your heart, soul, mind and strength, if you so choose; to love your neighbour as yourself; to offer your body as a living sacrifice to God; to love your fellow believers as Christ loves you. You are free because Jesus Christ has set you free.

Prayer: *Lord Jesus, thank you that knowing your truth sets me free.*

Twenty-Two

🔊

Friends Are Loved

He who loves me will be loved by my Father, and I too
will love him and show myself to him. (John 14:21)

As the Father has loved me, so have I loved you. Now
remain in my love. (John 15:9)

We can only love because He has first loved us. The
more you live in the revelation of God's love, the more you
will please Him by loving Him with all your heart, mind,
soul and strength!

It is both wonderful and extraordinary that Jesus should
say to us as His friends that He loves us in the same way as
the Father loves Him. He says that the Father loves Him
because He was obedient to His Father, and laid down His
life for His friends. He loves to see our obedience to Him,
therefore!

Jesus asked the people why they called Him 'Lord', but
did not do what He said! If He truly is your Lord, you are
happy to place your life under His direction. If you are
truly thankful that He laid His life down for you, then you
will lay down your life for others!

Does this mean that the Lord loves only those who obediently live their lives sacrificially? No, it is clear that He
loved us while we were still sinners by dying for us. He
loves all He has made, even those who reject Him and rebel
against Him. He tells us to love our enemies because He
loves His enemies! Yet, as the Father had a very special

57

relationship of love with His Son, so the disciples had a special relationship of love with Jesus because of their willingness to obey Him (albeit imperfectly) and to lay down their lives for others.

In other words, **Jesus has a special love for those who live as His friends. 'As the Father has loved me, so have I loved you. Abide in my love.'**

You do not have to do anything to win His love. Simply accept that He loves you and wants you to enter more and more deeply into that love, to be totally secure in that love, full of His love, and willing to give to others in the power of that love. He wants you to have a close, intimate relationship with Himself in which both the Father and the Son will come to make their home with you.

> If anyone loves me, he will obey my teaching. My Father will love him, and we will come to him and make our home with him. (John 14:23)

Prayer: *Lord Jesus, thank you that you love me.*

ॐ

Twenty-Three

Friends Are Given New Hearts

Just as Jesus's love for you is not based on sentiment or emotional feelings, so your love for Him does not have that basis either. Of course, you cannot love the Lord with all your soul without your emotions being involved. But your love for Him is birthed in your spirit rather than your soul!

God is Spirit. His love for you is born of the Spirit, but is to influence every part of your soul life (your mind, emotions and your will) and even your body.

Jesus humbled Himself, came as the willing servant of all, gave Himself unstintingly to the people. He washed the disciples' feet. He forgave people's sins and went to eat with sinners and outcasts. They flocked to hear Him because they realized that, instead of judging them as the religious leaders did, He loved them. Despite their unholiness, they did not shun the Holy One, but felt drawn to Him because of His love.

In loving the people in the way He did, Jesus was demonstrating His love for the Father, and the Father's love for the people. It was no burden to fulfil His Father's command to lay down His life as He did, because of the love in His own heart. **He wanted to obey His Father!**

If we love Jesus we want to obey Him and express His love to others. Only those who do not love do not want to obey. They dislike talk of obedience, and God's commands appear burdensome to them.

The Lord has given you a new heart and put His Spirit of love within you. Now He has written His law, not on a tablet of stone or in a book, but on your heart.

The promises God gave through the prophet Ezekiel have been fulfilled in Jesus:

> I will cleanse you from all your infirmities and from all your idols. I will give you a new heart and put a new spirit within you; I will remove from you your heart of stone and give you a heart of flesh. And I will put my Spirit in you and move you to follow my decrees and be careful to obey my laws. (Ezekiel 36:25–27)

These words refer to the new covenant of which you are a part. God gave you a new heart when you were born again. Before that time you walked in your own way and basically did what you wanted to do. Now, in the new life, you are able to obey the Lord and please Him because He has given you His own Spirit and written His commands on your new heart. You still have to choose to obey.

You will automatically obey His Word and live to please Him. This has to be a conscious daily decision on your part. Before your new birth you could only walk in the flesh (to please yourself). Now God has made it possible for you to walk in the Spirit (to please Him). You can do either. **You can choose to walk in the flesh, please yourself and grieve the Lord; or you can walk in the Spirit, obey His commands and please Him.**

There can be no doubt as to what He wants of His friends! Every day you will be faced with a series of decisions: self or other; self or obedience to Jesus; selfishness or selflessness.

To deny yourself without having the right heart, proves

to be impossible. No matter how hard you try, you inevitably fail!

Even new, clean hearts become dirty with use. This is why we need the Lord to cleanse and revive our hearts whenever we drift away from His best purposes. He is always ready to do this, and to give you every encouragement in fulfilling His Word.

Prayer: *Lord Jesus, thank you that you have given me a new heart.*

౩౽

Twenty-Four

৯৯

Friends Have Hearts
That Please the Lord

A pure heart pleases the Lord and leads to right attitudes and right motives, which in turn lead to right thinking and right actions.

To God, a pure heart is not only devoid of impurity, it is filled with the positive attributes of God's heart, a holy heart, a heart of love. It is a heart that prompts action, faith working through love. But the purity of the heart ensures the purity of motive. We can do many seemingly good things for the wrong motives. We can seek our own glory or reward. We can desire recognition from others, wanting to be praised for the things we do, upset when we do not receive the thanks or acclaim we think we deserve.

The ministries of some Christians are tainted by their need to be wanted. They do not serve because of the needs of those whom they serve, but because they are seeking their own fulfilment. Such people can be either overbearing or manipulative, often making others dependent on them because they have a need to be needed!

We want people to be Jesus-dependent, not minister-dependent, or counsellor-dependent. We have failed in ministry when we make people dependent on us, instead of on the truth that will set them free.

Some of those who complain about the demands that others make of them secretly enjoy the fact that they are wanted and needed. They would be devastated if nobody needed them! They create situations which ensure others need them, even though sometimes they claim they want to be rid of such responsibilities.

We cannot hide anything from the Lord, even the motives of our hearts: 'Surely you desire truth in the inner parts; you teach me wisdom in the inmost place' (Psalm 51:6). Nothing from outside can defile a person, only that which comes from within, from the heart! **When our hearts are filled with holy love, we give and serve willingly and joyfully, without any secret agenda of our own!**

A servant heart pleases the Lord. Those with servant hearts are quick to respond to need. They do not complain about what is asked of them; they are happy to serve. They welcome the opportunities to put their love into action, but do not want to take the glory to themselves; they are not looking for recognition. They are happy to serve for the sake of serving and fulfilling the need that is before them.

Serving comes naturally to those with servant hearts. They make themselves readily available when things need to be done and are happy to serve without complaining at the cost!

Everyone in Christian ministry needs a servant heart, no matter the nature of their ministry. **As every believer is to be in ministry (which simply means 'service'), every Christian needs a servant heart.** Jesus Himself has such a heart, and we are called to be as He is in the world! He came not to be served, but to serve and to give His life as a ransom for many.

Jesus pleased the Father, and it pleases Him to see the ways in which we reflect His heart and life! **A merciful heart pleases the Lord.** Jesus is merciful, always ready to forgive and to bless. It pleases Him when we forgive others, instead of harbouring grudges or any form of resentment, when we bless our enemies and those who hurt or wrong us.

The Lord's mercies are new every morning. There is not a day goes by that we do not need His mercy; and there is rarely a day when we do not need to extend mercy and forgiveness to others.

Our willingness to forgive comes from a right heart attitude. It is possible to react negatively to situations, and then remember we are to forgive. With the right attitude, you forgive instinctively as soon as anyone offends you.

It helps to remember how merciful Jesus has been to you in cancelling your debt towards God, taking upon Himself the punishment you deserved and letting you go free.

> For if you forgive men when they sin against you, your heavenly Father will also forgive you. But if you do not forgive men their sins, your Father will not forgive your sins. (Matthew 6:14–15)

Jesus teaches us to pray that God will forgive our trespasses **as we forgive those who trespass against us.** He gives us the parable of the Unmerciful Servant to show how essential it is to forgive. God has forgiven you and cancelled all your debt towards Him; you must therefore forgive all those who sin against you – a paltry debt by comparison.

In this parable the King is tender-hearted and therefore prepared to forgive the servant. This is an indispensable aspect of compassion that the Lord wants to see in our lives. **Instead of being hard-hearted, bitter and resentful towards others, we are to be tender-hearted, quick to forgive and to bless.**

Prayer: *Lord Jesus, I want to keep my heart pure and have a servant heart.*

Friends Have Thankful, Joyful Hearts

Those with hearts of thanksgiving and praise please Him. We are to rejoice in the Lord always. We are to give thanks in all circumstances, for this is His will for us in Christ Jesus. Those with hearts of praise react to trying circumstances with praise and rejoicing instead of grumbling and complaining! **Every positive attitude blesses the Lord, because He is so positive Himself!**

Paul learned to be content in all things and to bless the Lord on every occasion. He writes:

> Sing and make music in your hearts, always giving thanks to God the Father for everything, in the name of our Lord Jesus Christ. (Ephesians 5:19–20)

If you trust the Lord's sovereign oversight of your life, you will be thankful, no matter what the circumstances. He is always with you, the resources of heaven available to you. Negative situations are a testing of your faith, and by trusting in Him you will come through these tests.

While you resent a situation, the Lord seems to do precious little to change the circumstances. He waits until you give thanks, right in the middle of the turmoil, trauma or whatever else is happening. The reason for this is simple. While you resent the situation you are not lifting up the Lord Jesus over the circumstances. **As soon as you begin to thank Him, you are restoring Him to the place of**

honour and supremacy He needs to retain in your life.
When you stop looking to Him with thanksgiving, you are
looking somewhere else instead! Usually you look at yourself, and that is when you begin to react negatively, feeling
the situation has the better of you.

Thanking and praising the Lord are evidences of faith.
You look to Him, raise Him above the problems, realizing
He is far greater than any need that could ever arise in your
life. You thank Him that He is in charge; He knows your
circumstances, He loves you and wants to provide for you
in whatever way is necessary!

The theme of thanksgiving runs through Paul's letter to
the Colossians. He begins by saying:

> We always thank God, the Father of our Lord Jesus
> Christ, when we pray for you, because we have heard of
> your faith in Christ Jesus and of the love you have for all
> the saints. (Colossians 1:3–4)

You are to pray with thanksgiving, for you cannot pray
with faith without being thankful. When you pray, you are
to believe you have received whatever you ask. Unless you
can thank God for the answer, you do not expect to receive
the answer you need!

Paul prays that the Colossians may **joyfully give thanks**
to the Father who has qualified them to share in the inheritance of the saints in the Kingdom of light (Colossians
1:11–12). Joy and thanksgiving go together. Because you
are always to give thanks, you are always also to rejoice.
You will not always feel like doing this. There will be many
times when you will have to disregard your feelings in
order to obey!

When you least feel like praising God it is most important to do so. By doing this you enthrone Him afresh in your heart, right in the middle of the trying circumstances or negative feelings.

Paul goes on to say:

> So then, just as you received Christ Jesus as Lord, continue to live in him, rooted and built up in him, strengthened in the faith as you were taught, and overflowing with thankfulness. (Colossians 2:6–7)

You can only overflow when you are so full that you cannot possibly contain any more! This is how full of thanksgiving you are to be. Overflowing! To give thanks always becomes a way of life!

> And whatever you do, whether in word or deed, do it all in the name of the Lord Jesus Christ, giving thanks to God the Father through him. (Colossians 3:17)

Most believers have to fight certain negative attitudes. Fighting them may contain these attitudes, but does nothing to eliminate them. **Giving thanks eliminates the negative.** When you are positive there is no room for the negative!

> Be joyful always; pray continually; giving thanks in all circumstances, for this is God's will for you in Christ Jesus. (1 Thessalonians 5:16–18)

Speak God's blessing over your life and circumstances, instead of groaning and complaining about your situation. Speak His blessing over those around you. Pray His blessing over every area of concern. Be thoroughly positive. Thank the Lord that it is His purpose to bless you and lead you in His victorious procession in Christ.

Practise doing this every day. Persevere and you will see one situation after another changed by the grace of God. It is not enough to know this is what you should do! Do it! Give thanks always! Speak God's blessing over every situation!

Prayer: *Lord Jesus, I want to live with a thankful, joyful heart.*

༈

Twenty-Six

Friends Love

> Love is patient, love is kind. It does not envy, it does not
> boast, it is not proud. It is not rude, it is not self-seeking,
> it is not easily angered, it keeps no record of wrongs.
> Love does not delight in evil but rejoices with the truth.
> It always protects, always trusts, always hopes, always
> perseveres. Love never fails. (1 Corinthians 13:4–8)

Because Jesus has given His friends the life of His Spirit,
they have within them the qualities of His life and therefore
His love. Such love abides or remains for ever! At first sight
this seems an awesome list of attributes. We can see that
each was true of Jesus.

He was patient and kind. He was not envious of anyone.
He did not boast, nor was He proud. He was not rude, nor
self-seeking. He was not easily angered and kept no record
of wrongs. He never took delight in anything evil but came
to reveal the truth. He protected His loved ones, always
trusted the Father, always looked to the Father with hope.
He persevered through all the rejection, opposition and
persecution directed at Him. And His love never failed. He
demonstrated His love for the Father by fulfilling His will.

We are to be as He is in the world! However, if you place
yourself as the subject of these words, you do not get very
far before you feel like crying out to God for His forgiveness! For then you would say: 'I am patient, I am kind. I do

not envy, I do not boast, I am not proud. I am not rude. I am not self-seeking. I am not easily angered. I keep no record of wrongs. I do not delight in evil, but I rejoice with the truth. I always protect, I always trust, I always hope, I always persevere. My love never fails!'

No doubt you wish all those statements were a completely accurate description about you. Do not be discouraged! **This is the nature of the love Jesus has put in you by His Holy Spirit, and these qualities will be expressed through your life increasingly as you seek to live as a friend of Jesus.**

I have found it a useful exercise to use these verses in this personal way. I ask the Lord to forgive the ways in which I fail to reveal such love (which are many). **But I also speak these words over my life as a statement of faith, and pray that with His grace, the Lord will enable more and more of such love to be revealed in my life and ministry. You can do the same!**

It is important that we aim for the goals God sets for us in His Word. Never aim for anything less. He will enable us to go far beyond our natural accomplishments. And always be thankful for the progress that you are making as you allow the life of God's Spirit to be expressed through you more and more. Where you see areas of failure, ask Jesus for forgiveness and pray that He will release more of His love into your life.

It is not a matter of saying, 'Lord, please give me more patience', for patience is an expression of His love. It is love that is lacking. With more love there will inevitably be an increase in patience and of all the other qualities of His life!

Prayer: *Lord Jesus, help me to live a life of love.*

ʚϞ

Friends Are Patient

Love is patient. (1 Corinthians 13:4)

The Lord is infinitely patient with us because there is no end to His love. He is 'slow to anger, abounding in love' (Psalm 145:8). He does not treat us as we deserve, even though we fail so often to act in the love He wants of His friends. He extends His mercy to us every day when we turn to Him in repentance. He does not lecture us, but forgives and restores us.

Even when we sin in the same way again and again, and ask for His forgiveness as many times, still He does not become impatient. He waits until we have a genuine change of heart and no longer want to grieve Him in that way; until we are ready not only to ask for His forgiveness, but to turn away from that sin in true repentance. He forgives us and then completely delivers us from the power of that sin in our lives.

When we strive and struggle in our own strength, He stands patiently by, waiting for us to come to the end of ourselves and turn to Him for help! He is always ready. He is never worried when things seem to be in chaos and disorder, for He knows that He is in complete control and that He will bring order into the chaos as soon as we allow Him to do so!

Jesus demonstrated patience throughout His ministry, and He taught about patience in such parables as that of the Prodigal Son. When the younger son left home with his share of the inheritance, the father waited patiently for his return. He did not chase after him, for he knew the boy needed to work through his independence and rebellion and come to the end of himself, before he would have a genuine change of heart. His strong self-will and independence had to be broken before he would accept the father's love and respond to him in the right way!

With this process accomplished, the father welcomed him back with love and joy. The father is described as treating his younger son with compassion; literally, he was 'tender-hearted' towards him. Instead of reprimanding him, he lavished gifts on him and ordered a great celebration feast.

The older son was not at all forgiving or merciful. He was impatient with the father for even receiving his younger brother, and both resentful and jealous at the feast being given in his honour!

We become impatient when things do not go our way, according to our own plans and expectations. We grow impatient with those who do not agree with us. Impatience is clearly an expression of the flesh, and therefore is in opposition to the life of the Spirit.

Abraham inherited the promises of God 'by faith with patience'. The patience is usually the most difficult part! We want everything to be done immediately, or in our time; yet we will never succeed in rushing the Lord!

Paul was a man of great faith, and learned to be content in all circumstances. He knew that if God had promised to do something, He would certainly keep His word. He learned, therefore, not to be frustrated if things did not work out according to his own desires or time-scale.

If your heart is submitted to God and you trust Him, you know He is Lord of your circumstances and will be faithful to every promise He has given you; that you too can inherit God's promises by faith with patience.

Meanwhile do not allow others to disturb your peace. Jesus is bigger than any who cause you problems. He told Paul:

> My grace is sufficient for you; for my power is made perfect in weakness. (2 Corinthians 12:9)

God will give you grace to be patient; it is the fruit of the Holy Spirit who lives within you. Impatience, even with yourself, never accomplishes anything! Paul prayed that his readers might 'be strengthened with all power according to his glorious might so that you might have great endurance and patience', joyfully giving thanks to the Father (Colossians 1:11–12).

He wants you to give thanks in all circumstances, patiently trusting Him to fulfil all He has promised you.

Prayer: *Lord Jesus, thank you for your grace to enable me to live with patience.*

ℑℛ

Friends Are Kind

Love is kind. (1 Corinthians 13:4)

Kindness is another fruit of the Holy Spirit and therefore a characteristic of God's own heart. Jesus describes His Father as being 'kind to the ungrateful and wicked' (Luke 6:35). Even while we were still sinners He showed His loving kindness towards us by sending Jesus to die for us. In His great love He reaches out to sinners, even to those who hate Him!

If He has shown kindness to you when you did not deserve it, then you are to show kindness to others, irrespective of whether they deserve such kindness. If you have a kind heart, you will be kind, no matter what the circumstances or who the people involved. 'A kind man benefits himself' (Proverbs 11:17), while 'a kind-hearted woman gains respect' (Proverbs 11:16).

Kindness is a great encouragement to others. Think for a moment how appreciative you have been when others have shown you kindness, especially when you have been feeling really low.

An anxious heart weighs a man down, but a kind word cheers him up. (Proverbs 12:25)

Being kind to the needy is a form of giving, so the one who is kind will be blessed: 'Blessed is he who is kind to the needy' (Proverbs 14:21). 'Whoever is kind to the needy honours God' (Proverbs 14:31).

Such kindness is expressed in action, not simply in feeling sympathy for those in need. Jesus said:

> Then the King will say to those on his right, 'Come, you who are blessed by my Father; take your inheritance, the kingdom prepared for you since the creation of the world. For I was hungry and you gave me something to eat, I was thirsty and you gave me something to drink, I was a stranger and you invited me in, I needed clothes and you clothed me, I was sick and you looked after me, I was in prison and you came to visit me.'
> (Matthew 25:34–36)

This description of what will happen on the Day of Judgement shows not only how closely the Lord Himself identifies with those in need, but also how He rewards those who show His kindness to them. This is love in action – a good way to describe kindness!

No wonder Paul says: 'Be kind and compassionate to one another, forgiving each other, just as in Christ God forgave you' (Ephesians 4:32). This is the very opposite of being judgemental towards people and refusing to help them. 'Make sure that nobody pays back wrong for wrong, but always try to be kind to each other and to everyone else' (1 Thessalonians 5:15). Believers are to be kind to other believers, but also to others outside of the faith. As God's chosen ones we are to 'clothe ourselves with kindness' (Colossians 3:12).

To develop such kindness, ask the Lord to keep your heart full of love towards others, so that you react to situations in the right way.

How could the disciples be on the receiving end of some of the words of rebuke that Jesus spoke to them without being devastated as a result? They knew He loved them. They knew He had a tender compassionate heart. They experienced so much kindness that, when He needed to be tough, they could take it!

So even when things seem really difficult never lose sight of the tenderness and the loving-kindness of the Lord. He who is with you will surely help you. And then He will use you to help others.

Prayer: *Lord Jesus, I want to see your loving-kindness expressed in my life.*

Twenty-Nine

༈

Friends Do Not Envy

Love ... does not envy. (1 Corinthians 13:4)

You have no need to be envious. You have God as your
Father, Jesus as your Lord, the Holy Spirit living in you.
You are in Christ, and in Him you have received fullness of
life. You have been blessed in Him with every blessing in
heavenly places. He is the One who 'forgives all your sins
and heals all your diseases, who redeems your life from the
pit and crowns you with love and compassion, who satis-
fies your desires with good things so that your youth is re-
newed as the eagle's' (Psalm 103:3–5). **What could you
possibly be envious about? Or of whom could you be
envious? It is not possible for anyone to be blessed
more than God has chosen to bless you!**

When we look at others in envy, this is only because
we are guilty of unbelief. We think others have more than
we do, instead of being thankful for all that God has given
us and the rich inheritance we have in Christ. Envy is the
very opposite of rejoicing always and giving thanks in all
circumstances.

Like so many other sins it is easy to try to excuse ourselves. 'It is only natural,' we say. Or, 'I can't help reacting
in this way.' Sin is sin and is the evidence of an unclean
heart, for that is where the problem really lies. Don't be discouraged, our God is good at cleaning hearts! Of course,
you have to acknowledge your need and ask Him to

cleanse your heart. It is not only the present situation that He wishes to deal with; He wants to build the right dispositions into your heart so that on future occasions you will react in the right way too.

Sometimes you may be perplexed as to why God has allowed you to be in a situation which causes negative reactions. The situation did not cause the negativity, it only exposed what was already in your heart. Nothing from outside is able to defile a person, Jesus teaches us. It is only what is already in the heart that causes someone to be unclean!

Instead of being resentful, thank the Lord that He has allowed the problem to arise to show you what is still there within you needing to be dealt with. And know that once it has been exposed, the Lord is ready to do something about it!

James describes envy as being 'earthly, unspiritual, of the devil. For where you have envy and selfish ambition, there you find disorder and every evil practice' (James 3:15–16). This is strong language! Notice how he links envy and selfish ambition, the desire to raise yourself above others. This is the consequence of being envious and proud. This is a fleshly and self-defeating attitude, for the Lord pulls down the proud, but lifts up the humble.

When you detect any trace of envy, instead of being resentful give thanks that the other people are blessed. Praise God for what He is doing in them. Be positive, and the negative reaction cannot last.

Many Christians make the mistake of fighting the flesh, the self-life, instead of denying it. There is a big difference between those two approaches. Whenever you fight your desires you only succeed in stirring them up still further!

Those who walk in the Spirit will not gratify the desires of the flesh, Paul says. **Do the very opposite to the fleshly reaction.** When the flesh wants to judge, forgive. When your self-life feels envious, give thanks. **Then you have won the victory and you have refused to become the victim of negative reactions and emotions.**

At first it may seem unreal as you do this. You might even feel hypocritical because, although you are giving thanks, you know well that you do not feel thankful. If you persist, your emotions will catch up with your lips! The alternative is to fall into a negative mood of anger, bitterness and resentment, the fruit of envy. Better to rejoice and give thanks!

Prayer: *Lord Jesus, thank you, thank you, thank you, for all you have done for me and given me.*

🔊

Thirty

ॐ

Friends Do Not Boast

Love … does not boast. (1 Corinthians 13:4)

Everything God has done for you and all that He has given you is a result of His grace. So what do you have to boast about? Everything you achieve in God, all the fruit you produce, is the result of His Spirit working within you. So what do you have to boast about? Every spiritual gift, every blessing, comes from Him. So what do you have to boast about? Every healing, every demonstration of His power, is for His glory. So what do you have to boast about? Every way in which He uses you is the result of His grace. So what do you have to boast about? Every sinner who turns to the Lord is a product of the convicting and transforming power of the Holy Spirit. So what do you have to boast about?

You are prone to sin and fail, despite all the Lord has done for you. So what do you have to boast about? You miss many opportunities to express His love and power to others. So what do you have to boast about? You too often choose your own way above His and do not believe the words of promise He gives you. So what do you have to boast about? You are completely dependent on His love, grace and mercy. So what do you have to boast about?

There are only two ways in which you should boast. Paul says:

'Let him who boasts boast in the Lord.' For it is not the one who commends himself who is approved, but the one whom the Lord commends.
(2 Corinthians 10:17–18)

Because the Lord is the only one to whom glory belongs for all that He has done, our boast is of Him, and only of Him. Paul also says: 'May I never boast except in the cross of our Lord Jesus Christ, through which the world was crucified to me, and I to the world' (Galatians 6:14). Paul had many natural gifts. God had used him in wonderful ways; yet he knew all the glory was the Lord's. He still regarded himself as the chief of sinners because he had persecuted the Church. Because Jesus accomplished everything for him on the cross, making it possible for him to be forgiven, accepted and to become a child of His Kingdom, Paul's boast was in the cross, in what had been done for him by Jesus.

The same is true for you. You have done nothing of which you have any right to boast. **Everything you have accomplished in Christ is the result of the working of His Spirit in and through you; and so all the glory rightly goes to the Lord!**

For it is by grace you have been saved, through faith – and this is not from yourselves, it is the gift of God – not by works, so that no one can boast. (Ephesians 2:8–9)

Does this mean you are never to boast about yourself? Well, Paul says there is another way to boast, and that is about your weaknesses! He lived constantly aware of his own weakness, yet more aware of the power of Christ that could work through him. Jesus had told him that His power is made perfect in weakness; so Paul concluded:

Therefore I will boast all the more gladly about my weaknesses, so that Christ's power can rest on me. That is why for Christ's sake, I delight in weaknesses, in insults, in hardships, in persecutions, in difficulties. For when I am weak, then I am strong. (2 Corinthians 12:9–10)

This is not the negative unbelief of someone who constantly speaks about his or her inability to do anything, or be used by God in any significant way. What Paul says is a statement of strong faith. He is saying that no matter how great his weakness, God is able to use him mightily. **The same is true for you! Delight in your weaknesses and give all the glory to the Lord for what He accomplishes through you!**

We even have to be careful not to boast of others whom the Lord uses greatly, for this steals some of the glory from God, taking the focus away from Him and putting it on the servant instead. This can easily lead to pride in the servant, which is the quickest way to compromise the way in which God is using him or her.

Testimony can be used by the Lord to point others to Christ. But even in the giving of testimony we have to be careful not to boast. It is easy to thank the Lord for what He has done, while making the point that it was you He used, or you who was particularly blessed, thus giving the impression that you are someone special, apart from others. **The more humility there is in a testimony, the more powerful it is as a witness to others, for then Christ comes shining through the words that are spoken!**

Prayer: *Lord Jesus, my boast is in you and in you alone.*

𝄞

Thirty-One

Friends Are Not Proud

Love … is not proud. (1 Corinthians 13:4)

Boasting is a form of pride. And pride is a heart attitude that lies behind most sin. Most of us find other proud people objectionable, while remaining blind to our own pride!

There are two kinds of proud people. First, the arrogant. These are most readily recognized as being proud. Whether real or imagined, they flaunt their achievements before others. They draw attention to themselves and their abilities. They have an exalted idea of their importance and are quick to judge and criticize others whom they regard as lesser mortals! The proud cannot understand if their gifts are not recognized and applauded by everyone else.

Spiritual arrogance results in people thinking they have superior faith to others, or they are more loving or generous. It was the Pharisees who flaunted their giving before men. The arrogant want everyone to know what they are doing for the Lord and for others, and they expect to be applauded for their efforts!

The second kind of proud person is not so easily recognized as such. Pride draws attention to self, and there are those who do this through inverted pride. Instead of drawing attention to their gifts, their abilities and accomplishments, they draw attention to their failure and inadequacy. They talk about themselves, not arrogantly, but negatively.

Nevertheless, self still is very much the focus of their attention.

Such people are often manipulative and want to gain attention by suggesting they are not really loved or wanted. They want to appear humble, and often think they are, whereas in fact they are full of self and spend most of their time thinking about themselves.

This is totally different from the way in which Paul boasted about his weaknesses. He saw those as an opportunity to prove the power of God and be mightily used by Him. Those with inverted pride have their confidence in themselves and their own lack of ability. There is little or no expectation that God is going to do great things in their lives, or use them in any significant way.

Proud people want to be loved – both the arrogant and those with inverted pride – but do little to love others. Concentration on self seriously limits their ability to love. Often when they do love others, they have a hidden agenda. They expect to benefit from what they do, either by the recognition they receive or because they can expect something in return! It is difficult for them to love with pure motives, because they are so obsessed with self.

Friends of Jesus should be neither arrogant, nor those with a negative self-image. Jesus will exalt them in the right way when they walk humbly before Him and others. They want to glorify Him, not draw attention to themselves.

Prayer: *Lord Jesus, I want to walk humbly before you and before others.*

Thirty-Two

ॐ

Friends Are Not Rude
or Self-Seeking

Love … is not rude. It is not self-seeking.
(1 Corinthians 13:5)

Love is not rude. When you love others, you show you care about them, you recognize their worth and want to encourage and affirm them. Rudeness is the very opposite. It is self-assertive. It demeans others. It is an aspect of pride in that it exalts self over and above others.

It may seem that rudeness is effective in getting your way, especially when dealing with the world. However, love will always accomplish more. **People react negatively to rudeness because it is crushing in its effect on them; they respond positively to love, because it encourages them. People operate more effectively when they are encouraged than when they are made to feel small.**

Christians are not to operate as the world does, anyway! The world will not believe unless we show the life of which we speak. If we live as the world lives, how will people know the true life and value of God's Kingdom?

Any form of self-seeking is the opposite of love. Paul speaks of selfish ambition as being a work of the flesh and says that 'those who live like this will not inherit the kingdom of God' (Galatians 5:21). He also says:

> **Do nothing out of selfish ambition or vain conceit,
> but in humility count others better than yourselves.
> Each of you should look not only to your own inter-
> ests, but also to the interests of others**.
> (Philippians 2:3–4)

Rudeness and self-seeking suggest you are better or more
important than others; they certainly are not expressions of
preferring others above yourself. Such things, James says,
lead to disorder and every evil practice. They do not, therefore, belong to the lifestyle of the friends of Jesus! The
wisdom that God gives is very different:

> But the wisdom that comes from heaven is first of all
> pure; then peace-loving, considerate, submissive, full of
> mercy and good fruit, impartial and sincere.
> (James 3:17)

Now that does sound like a good description of a friend of
Jesus!

**Every expression of God's love will be positive, be-
cause there are no negatives in Him.** The purpose of His
Spirit living within you is to eliminate the negative things
that affect both you and those you influence. All the fruit of
the Holy Spirit is positive. The life of God's Kingdom is
positive. It is not difficult to see whether you are being
negative or positive at any given moment.

Love is positive, as are joy, peace, hope, power, goodness, kindness, forgiveness, mercy, grace, compassion,
healing. Every aspect of the enemy's life is negative: lying,
deception, stealing, oppression, bondage, resentment,
aggression, spite, pride, selfishness, sickness and so on.

Sometimes we blind ourselves to the truth because we

do not want to face its implications. This is certainly the case with self-seeking. Love of self tempts us to feel justified in seeking our own objectives. We feel right about our negative reactions and judgements of others. If we are not careful this will also blind us to the effects our selfishness has on others around us. A selfish person will not care about this because he is more intent on pleasing himself than being concerned about others. **A friend of Jesus wants to express God's love to others, not his own selfishness!**

Self gets; love gives. So, for example, lust is a self-seeking gratification of desires, whereas love places concern for others above self.

Can we ever eradicate this self element completely? We would be perfect in every expression of our lives if we did so. We really would love like Jesus did! This must be our aim, even if we do not always hit the mark!

Because of the nature of the essential selfishness of your self life, Jesus says that any who follow Him will have to deny themselves and take up their cross daily in order to follow Him. Either you will seek to fulfil His purposes of love, or you will seek to gratify your desires and fulfil your own plans instead. You cannot do both, because His nature is so intrinsically different from the flesh.

He is love; and love is not self-seeking!

Prayer: *Lord Jesus, I want to be like you in seeking the welfare of others above myself.*

৩৯

Thirty-Three

Friends Keep No Record of Wrongs

Love ... is not easily angered, it keeps no record of
wrongs. (1 Corinthians 13:5)

All the qualities of love Paul mentions are linked. The Lord
is not going to promote selfishness, envy, pride or any
other negative desire. **His Spirit will work in us all the
positive attributes of His love.**

Your flesh becomes easily angered when you do not get
your own way. You can exhibit this anger or suppress it,
but it is there, part of your fleshly nature. The Spirit works
in you God's patience and long-suffering. You have both
Spirit and flesh. It is always a matter of which of the two
you are going to please.

The flesh does not want to forgive, it is by nature bitter
and resentful, which are negative emotions. The Spirit
urges you to forgive, and reminds you of the dire consequences of refusing to do so. Because the Lord forgives
you, He expects you to forgive others!

When the Lord forgives you, He eradicates from the
record books in heaven every record of the sins He forgives. So it is worth being specific when you ask Him to
forgive you! The Lord will not hold against you anything
He has forgiven, either now or in the future. There will be
no mention on the Day of Judgement of the sins He has
eradicated. He does not forgive on a temporary basis: 'I forgive you now, but just wait until the Day of Judgement!'

You don't need to fear that those forgiven sins will again be held against you. Jesus has already suffered the punishment you deserved. **Those forgiven sins are gone for ever. They are eradicated from the record books in heaven!**

Because you are to forgive in the same way that Jesus has forgiven you, you are to keep no record of wrongs! You are not to forgive superficially, while continuing to harbour resentment inwardly. You should not even allow your relationships with those who have sinned against you to be affected, once you have forgiven them. You are to keep no record of wrongs, even in your mind. Certainly you are not to seek revenge for the negative things you have suffered through others. If Jesus is prepared to forgive and forget, that is precisely what you are to do. This is not necessarily easy, and sometimes you have to work through a series of negative emotions and reactions before your attitude towards those who have offended you is positive and loving.

Forgiveness is first and foremost a decision, not an emotion. You choose to forgive. Once the decision is made, the emotions will catch up with the decision of your will. If you wait for the right feelings you may never forgive! **The act of the will comes before, not after, the right feelings.**

No matter what the situation, you can forgive. You are free to exercise your will in any way you choose. **You can choose to forgive, or you can refuse to do so.**

Basically, forgiveness is a matter of your heart attitudes. I have been deeply moved by testimonies of Christians who have forgiven those who have murdered their loved ones. I have known them to visit them in prison, praying for them to come to faith in Jesus. This is the right, good and positive reaction in the most dire circumstances that must delight the Lord, and is a great witness not only to the murderers, but to the world generally.

You are no doubt very glad that the Lord keeps no record of your forgiven sins. **So do not keep a record of those sins you have forgiven.** Pray for those who have rejected, persecuted, offended or even abused you, speaking blessing over their lives. Be thankful for the grace Jesus gives you to do this. Like Him, you can pray: 'Father, forgive them, they do not know what they are doing.' Let no root of bitterness grow up within you! **Forgive, even as Christ has forgiven you!**

Prayer: *Lord Jesus, I choose to forgive all who have ever wronged me.*

5♫

Friends Rejoice in the Truth

Love ... does not delight in evil but rejoices with the truth. (1 Corinthians 13:6)

The flesh delights in evil. So Hollywood fills our cinema and TV screens with violence, lust and horror, as film-makers pander to people's fleshly desires. The flesh is curious about the occult and other supernatural manifestations of the devil. Newspapers and magazines are filled with gossip because of the lurid interest in others' sins.

People like to spread rumour and scandal, regardless of whether what they relate is true or not. Some make it sound as if they deplore such sins, while rejoicing at every opportunity to talk about them!

All these are evidences of the fact that the flesh delights in evil. It is not only intrinsically evil people who do this. Love of sin is the nature of the flesh life. Such attitudes are the very opposite of love and therefore of the way in which Christians are to walk. 'Love does not delight in evil but re-joices with the truth.'

Gossips may say they are concerned only to speak of things that are true about other people. This is **not** what Paul means when he talks of rejoicing with the truth. Even if you have true information about others' sins and failings, this is no excuse for spreading such information. If you for-give, you forget. **As long as you speak of the issues concerned, you have certainly not forgotten them, and**

therefore have not forgiven them. When you sin you want others to forgive you, not talk about your sins to others!

When you rejoice in the truth you rejoice about Jesus. You rejoice that He keeps no record of wrongs, that when He forgives He puts all your sins behind His back, and chooses never to hold those things against you!

The truth is the same for everyone. When you rejoice in the truth, you rejoice in all Jesus has accomplished for you and the inheritance He has given you. Delight in every opportunity you have to share that truth with others, to be used by God to guide others to the truth that will set them free and cause them to rejoice in what Jesus has done for them.

The truth is always right! God will not change or compromise that truth for you or for anyone. It remains constant for all time!

The more your heart is in line with God's heart, the more you will rejoice in the truth instead of delighting in evil! Be thankful for the ways in which you have changed already, losing your desire for many of the things that displease your Lord, rejoicing instead in the things that please Him!

Be thankful that He has made you a child of the truth. John says:

> It gave me great joy to have some brothers come and tell about your faithfulness to the truth and how you continue to walk in the truth. I have no greater joy than to hear that my children are walking in the truth.
> (3 John 3–4)

Prayer: *Lord Jesus, I delight in you and in the truth of your Word.*

Thirty-Five

5ᘒ

Friends Always Protect

Love … always protects. (1 Corinthians 13:7)

Those who love the Lord will also love one another! They will love others as He has loved them!

It must offend God to hear His children slandering one another, instead of walking in the truth. Sadly, the Church does not have the record of godliness it should have in this respect. It is all too common to hear Christians criticizing and judging one another. There is too much gossip among believers; too much rejoicing in evil, especially when a brother falls from grace in some way. There is too much negative back-biting. None of these things reveal love! The very opposite, in fact!

The Lord protects those He loves. He is the One who is able to keep us from falling. He is our shield and defence. He is a wall of protection around us. He does not rejoice when we fall foul of some snare of the enemy, neither does He spread gossip about His children around His family. He does not even want to do such things. He works for our welfare, not to damage or criticize us.

If we love, we will not only avoid speaking negatively and critically of each other, but we will protect others; we will work for their good. We will refuse to listen to gossip. We will be quick to defend each other against any other form of verbal attack. We will speak positively of them, even when we do not agree with them.

You may not agree with other brethren over every point of doctrine. You may even think they are misguided and cause harm by the things they preach and teach. This is never an excuse to speak evil of those brothers, for despite your differences, they are your brothers and friends of Jesus! You may disagree publicly with what you consider wrong doctrine, but without criticizing the brother who holds those doctrines!

I believe that some brethren teach things that put people into bondage instead of bringing them into the freedom and release which is God's will for all His children. Sometimes in my ministry it is necessary to speak against what I believe to be wrong doctrine, but never against the brethren who hold those doctrines. I am careful to avoid mentioning any brother or sister by name. It is far more important to preach the truth positively, for when people have a grasp of the truth, they will see for themselves what conflicts with that truth!

Love protects, even those you do not agree with! It is better to pray for your brethren than to criticize them. Ask the Lord to keep them and protect them from every form of evil or deception; 'for he is able to keep all that is entrusted to him day by day'. Pray the Lord's richest favour upon them and seek to be a blessing to them.

In His love for you, the Lord protects you far more than you realize. He has often protected you from evil, without you being aware of the fact. **He protects His friends and He wants you to do the same!**

Prayer: *Lord Jesus, I will use my mouth to bless.*

Thirty-Six

5ဂ

Friends Trust, Hope and Persevere

Love … always trusts, always hopes, always perseveres.
(1 Corinthians 13:7)

'Love always trusts.' Those who abide in Jesus's love trust Him! Love and trust go together. Faith working through love!

In human relationships the same principle is true, for trust is an important aspect of love. If we are to love one another, we are therefore to trust one another. It is one thing to trust the Lord, who never fails us and whose love is perfect; but are we really expected to trust others who are fallible, and whose love is often tainted by selfish motives?

It is not wise to place yourself in a position of vulnerability with those who are not to be trusted, to confide in those who will gossip about you! Neither is it wise to place yourself under leaders who are not truly spiritual! You cannot trust such leaders to lead you in the way God intends. He does not encourage us to be foolish, but urges us to be wise.

The people that are trustworthy are those who hold to the truth. They teach the truth, they believe the truth, they live by the truth. Their lives demonstrate the truth. They hold to the truth, even in adverse circumstances. Knowing the truth sets them free and holding fast to the truth enables them to maintain that freedom.

Because the believer is always to trust in the truth, he or she is always to be full of hope. The things for which we hope are those things the Lord promises to do in the future. Because it is the Lord who has promised those things, there is no question as to whether they will come about, or not. If the Lord has spoken, they will surely happen! Hope does not disappoint us.

Love always hopes. You need never be despondent because all God's promises for His children are good and are given us in Christ. He is the 'Yes', the 'Amen' to all God's promises.

Often the circumstances we face seem to indicate the very opposite to what God has promised us. At such times we have to hold fast to God's Word in the face of those adverse circumstances. We hold on to our hope, knowing that God will surely do what He has promised, even if He has to turn the whole situation completely around!

We do not hope sometimes; we hope always. We never lose hope. We are always positive in our attitudes. We do not speak negatively of our situation, therefore, for this would indicate an absence of hope. 'Love always perseveres.' James says:

> Consider it pure joy, my brothers, whenever you face trials of many kinds, because you know that the testing of your faith produces perseverance. Perseverance must finish its work so that you may be mature and complete, not lacking anything. (James 1:2–4)

Perseverance is an important indication of your love for the Lord, for it demonstrates that you trust Him. You do not need much trust when things are easy, but determination and perseverance are required if you are to maintain your trust and persevere in hope when every-thing seems against you. Such perseverance is a sign of spiritual maturity. You refuse to give up easily as those who follow their feelings often do. James says further:

> Blessed is the man who perseveres under trial, because when he has stood the test, he will receive the crown of life that God has promised to those who love him. (James 1:12)

Perseverance brings about two wonderful results. It produces the maturity which results in you not lacking anything now! And you will receive the crown of life. It has very important consequences in your life, now and eternally!

As a friend of Jesus, always persevere in your love and trust. Jesus is always to be trusted. His love for you will never fail and He will bring you to the fulfilment of all He has promised you. To Him be all the glory!

Prayer: *Lord Jesus, please give me the grace to persevere in faith, to believe your Word above my circumstances.*

᠄

Thirty-Seven

ॐ

Friends Know That Love Never Fails

Love never fails. (1 Corinthians 13:8)

Many things in life are unstable and uncertain. One thing is absolutely sure: **God's love for you is eternal; it will never change or fail.** He is always reliable, and His Word thoroughly trustworthy!

Likewise, the love He has put in you will never fail! It is important to realize this. The enemy tries to sow seeds of doubt in your mind. If he cannot do this about present circumstances, he will try to make you have doubts about the future. He wants you to fear that you will fail the Lord in the future. This is in direct contradiction to Jesus's command not to take any thought about tomorrow.

You are to live in love and trust, not fear, especially fear of some imagined situation that may never come about anyway. Some Christians fear they might deny the Lord if they had to suffer persecution or physical torture for their faith. **God gives you the grace you need for each day, which is why He tells you not to worry about tomorrow. Tomorrow He will give you sufficient grace for tomorrow.** Whatever the future holds, He will give you the grace to face the demands made on you.

Today you do not have the grace for tomorrow, because you do not need such grace today! Do not listen to any false fears dreamed up by your own imagination. **The Lord will never fail you, and He will work in you the grace to**

ensure that you will not fail Him. Whenever you have trusted in Him in the past, He has never allowed you to fail. And how many occasions have there been when you have feared a situation, only to find that your fears were completely unfounded! Your imagination ran riot, concentrating on the negative things you feared might happen!

There is no fear in love; the perfect love of God casts out all fear.

When we love others we will not fail them either, at least not intentionally. There are times when we inadvertently fail those we love, and those who love us fail us too. At such times we need to be forgiven and to forgive those who have failed us. Where people love one another such reconciliation is usually not difficult.

When we trust to the resources of the Holy Spirit, we will not fail to express the love required of us. **We cannot do in our own strength what God has designed to be accomplished only in the power of the Spirit He has given us!** He has put into you the love that never fails. Your own human love is weak; His love in you is strong!

Prayer: *Lord Jesus, thank you that your love for me never fails.*

♋

Thirty-Eight

Jesus Shepherds His Friends

> The Lord is my shepherd, I shall not want. He makes me lie down in green pastures, he leads me beside still waters, he restores my soul. He guides me in paths of righteousness for his name's sake. (Psalm 23:1–3)

Jesus leads His friends; He is their Shepherd who cares for them!

These well-known words of David face us with some profound truths. To understand their full impact, we need to realize that in lands such as Israel, the shepherd has to lead his flock, walking ahead of them for several miles every day to find sufficient pasture. He cannot leave them in a lush field to look after themselves!

If the Lord is your Shepherd, you will not want. You can know that the Lord is the Shepherd without actually allowing Him to shepherd you! But if you take Him as your personal Shepherd, then what was true for David becomes true for you: you will lack nothing!

Jesus was Lord long before you recognized Him as such. He died on the cross as your Saviour long before you were born! There came the moment when you acknowledged that He is not only Lord, but your Lord. **You took Him to be your Lord personally.** You recognized He had died for **you** and **He became your personal Saviour.** Then you were able to benefit from all He had done on the cross.

He is the Lord your Healer. You can know He is able to

heal, and you can ask Him to heal you, but without really having taken Him as your personal Healer. The Lord wants you to take Him as your Healer, your health and salvation; to have a continual relationship in which you look to Him to keep you in good health.

The Lord also reveals Himself as your Provider. You can ask Him to provide without having necessarily taken Him as your personal Provider! Expect Him to provide for you continually. Do not wait for need to arise before looking to Him for provision!

David's statement in Psalm 23 signifies that He related to the Lord as His personal Shepherd. 'The Lord is **my** Shepherd'. He therefore comes to the conclusion, 'I shall not want.' If the Lord was David's personal Shepherd, He would care for him. He would never leave him in need. He would lack nothing.

Furthermore, David appreciated that the Lord would exercise the role of the Shepherd in leading him. This proved to be very important in the years following, for although David had great promises from God, it often seemed that his circumstances belied the promises. He was able to trust that the Lord would lead him through all the adverse experiences into the fulfilment of the promises He had given him.

'He leads me beside still waters.' The Lord led him through times of turmoil to places of peace. 'He guides me in paths of righteousness.' Later David was to sin grievously; yet instead of judging him and putting him to one side, the Lord restored his soul and led him again in the paths of righteousness!

As his Shepherd, the Lord caused David to lie down in green pastures, a luxury in a semi-arid land. The Lord wanted His servant to prosper! He did not need to fear any kind of evil. Even though he might have to walk through a valley of deep darkness, his Shepherd would be with him! Goodness and love would follow him all the days of his life.

All this and much more was apparent to David because he had taken the Lord as his personal Shepherd.

As His friend, the Lord also wants you to look to Him as your Shepherd. All these things can become personal revelation for **you**. He will care for **you** so that **you** will lack nothing. He will lead **you** to places of peace, even if you have to go through a period of turmoil. He will cause **you** to lie down in green pastures. He will lead **you** in paths of righteousness, for His own sake, so that His purposes for **you** can be fulfilled.

You will not need to fear any evil because your Shepherd is always with you. Goodness and love will follow you all the days of **your** life. **He will anoint your head with the oil of His Spirit so that your cup overflows!**

The more you lay hold of the personal attributes of Jesus's character and make them your own by faith, the more you will be able to live in the glorious inheritance He has prepared for you!

Jesus describes Himself as 'the good Shepherd'. He knows His sheep and they know Him. He knows **you** and by His grace **you** have come to know Him.

He lays down His life for the sheep; so He has laid down His life for you. His sheep 'follow him because they know his voice' (John 10:4). **You** can know His voice because He has put His Spirit in **you**, and **you** are able to follow Him. As you do so, all the promises David experiences will be yours also. Jesus will care for **you**, even if you have to pass through the valley of deepest darkness. **You** will never need to fear, for the Shepherd is with you.

Not only does He want all His sheep to know Him, recognize His voice and follow Him; He also desires that the sheep recognize their unity under the One Shepherd. He wants them to affirm one another, not be at odds with each other; to love one another as He has loved them.

> I have other sheep that are not of this sheep pen. I must bring them also. They too will listen to my voice, and there shall be one flock and one shepherd. (John 10:16)

All the friends of Jesus are His sheep. Despite our differences, we are all sheep under the one Shepherd. He will not lead us in a thousand different directions at the same time. Rather, He draws us together in His global plan.

You are a part of that plan. Jesus wants you to recognize your unity with all the other friends of Jesus, to cooperate with them in preparing for Him to come again in triumph. Before that event the Church is to demonstrate the life of which the Gospel speaks: a unity that is the result of Christians' love for Jesus and for one another. This is why Jesus prayed that all His disciples would be one; for then the world would know that He is the Christ, the Messiah, and that He loves us in just the same way that the Father loved Him!

Prayer: *Lord Jesus, thank you for being my Shepherd.*

ॐ

Thirty-Nine

ॐ

Jesus Provides for His Friends

God, who richly provides us with everything for our enjoyment. (1 Timothy 6:17)

When you love someone you are concerned for their welfare in every respect. The Lord is our Provider because He would not truly love us unless He was prepared to provide for us. To doubt His willingness to provide is to question His love!

John tells us that if our love for one another is genuine, we will love in action, not just with words. If this true for us, it is supremely true of Jesus. He does not want to love us only with words of encouragement, but with action. He showed this to the ultimate by giving His life for us on the cross. If He was prepared to make that supreme sacrifice, then He is certainly prepared to give to us in lesser ways!

John asks how it could be possible to have this world's goods, to see a brother in need, and yet close your heart towards that brother! To do that would indicate that the love of God could not be in you, he says! The reason for this is simple. Love is expressed in giving. If God loves, therefore, He wants to give to us. **If the Lord expects us to love others by giving to them, then it is obvious that He will express His love for us in giving to us!**

You are not to love Him, however, for what you can get out of Him! Nevertheless to know the Lord is to know you can receive from His abundance. You can never give to

Him or to one of His children, without Him giving much more back to you! He will never allow you to outdo Him in giving, because His love is so much greater than your love. He gives back 'good measure, pressed down, shaken together and running over'!

The Lord teaches us principles of giving that have a profound effect on those who are faithful in putting them into practice. Jesus says you reap what you sow. The measure you use in giving to others will determine the measure used to give back to you.

Everything we receive from the Lord is still a work of His grace. We cannot earn His blessings by our giving, and we will never deserve to receive anything from Him. But there is no end to His grace!

> For you know the grace of our Lord Jesus Christ, that though he was rich, yet for your sakes he became poor, so that you through his poverty might become rich.
> (2 Corinthians 8:9)

Although Paul says this within the context of the giving of money, he is clearly speaking of a principle that relates to all Jesus has done for us, and not only about money. The reason for Jesus becoming poor was to make us rich – in every way. This is the outworking of His grace. He wants to give and give and give to His beloved ones. And so John gives this testimony:

> From the fullness of his grace we have all received one blessing after another. (John 1:16)

This was the apostles' experience, both during Jesus's earthly ministry and subsequent to His resurrection and return to heaven.

Jesus wants you to receive one blessing after another because of His wonderful grace. It is not that He gets caught up in a 'blessing syndrome'; but in His wisdom He knows that the more you receive from Him, the more you will have to give. **You cannot give what you have not first received yourself.**

Jesus does not mind how much blessing He pours into the lives of His friends. The more He can give the better, for then they will be more effective in giving the evidences of His love to others. Paul puts it this way:

> And God is able to make all grace abound to you, so that in all things at all times, having all that you need, you will abound in every good work. (2 Corinthians 9:8)

He wants you to have **all** that you need! He loves you; He is your Shepherd and Provider. He wants to give and give and give to you. He knows that you will then be able 'to abound in every good work'. You will be able to give and give and give to others. And the more you give, the more you will receive. Then you will have even more to give; and then God will give more back to you. Then you will have still more to give; and God will give still more to you – and so on!

It defeats God's intention if you do not believe He wants to give to you and meet all your needs according to the glorious riches He has given in Christ Jesus.

> Now he who supplies seed to the sower and bread for food will also supply and increase your store of seed and will increase the harvest of your righteousness. You will be made rich in every way so that you can be generous on every occasion, and through us your generosity will result in thanksgiving to God. (2 Corinthians 9:10–11)

The Lord's purpose is that 'you will be made rich in every way', but not to feed your selfishness; rather, to make you generous on every occasion! For then you will reflect an essential characteristic of God – His grace. He wants to make you gracious, generous!

> I always thank God for you because of his grace given you in Christ Jesus. For in him you have been enriched in every way – in all your speaking and in all your knowledge – because our testimony about Christ was confirmed in you. (1 Corinthians 1: 4–6)

This is the effect of His grace, which is available to every believer. He does not want you to doubt His willingness to supply your every need. Neither does He want you to miss the opportunities He gives you to be a blessing to others by the way in which He can use you to give to them, of yourself, your time, abilities, money and resources. **The greater the blessing you are to others, the more you will be blessed.**

So take the Lord as your personal Provider. Know that He will always provide for you as you obey Him in giving to others. As you seek first His Kingdom and righteousness, everything else will be added to you!

Prayer: *Lord Jesus, thank you that you want to bless me.*

🔊

Forty

Jesus Heals His Friends

'I am the Lord, who heals you' or 'I am the Lord your healer'. (Exodus 15:26)

Jesus spent a good deal of His ministry healing people. When He sent His disciples out to proclaim the Gospel of the Kingdom, He commanded them to heal the sick. It has always been God's nature to heal!

Jesus is your health and your salvation. The word 'salvation' means 'healing'. As His friend, He is concerned about your health in spirit, soul and body. He wants to heal you physically as well as spiritually. Your body is an important part of you! You could not exist without it. Your body is a temple of the Holy Spirit. You cannot love, care or witness to others without your body. So it would be almost blasphemous to suggest that God is only concerned about your soul, but not your body.

Healing was one of the gifts given to the Church through the Holy Spirit. He has lost none of His power! He is as powerful today as in New Testament times! God's commission to His Church has not changed, either. 'Heal the sick' is still the Lord's command to His followers.

The problem many have with healing comes from experience; not every one who prays to be healed is healed. To effect God's purposes we need to operate in faith and with the authority He gives us. Jesus says we are not to doubt the outcome when we pray, but are to believe we have received whatever we ask in prayer.

It is difficult to expect God to heal, to have no doubt about the outcome, unless you are thoroughly convinced from God's Word that it is His purpose to heal you. He wants you to live in the revelation that He is your Healer, your health and your salvation. You are living in the Healer and He in you. Your expectation is that you will live in His health, not in sickness.

However, He does not condemn any believer for being sick. Sin is not God's purpose for any of His children. Yet, when we sin, He does not throw us out of His Kingdom. He forgives and restores us instead of condemning us. When we are sick, He does not judge us for being sick. Instead He extends His love and compassion to us. He is ready to release His power into our lives in response to our faith, and to glorify His name by the work of healing He does within us!

On the cross, Jesus dealt with every negative that can afflict our lives: 'By his wounds we are healed' (Isaiah 53:5). Matthew knew this Scripture referred to the healing of physical sickness and deliverance from demonic powers, as well as the healing of emotional and spiritual needs.

> When evening came, many who were demon-possessed were brought to him, and he drove out the spirits with a word and healed all their sick. This was to fulfil what was spoken through the prophet Isaiah: 'He took up our infirmities and carried our diseases.' (Matthew 8:16–17)

As a friend of Jesus, take Him as your health, your salvation, your Healer! Know that in His love for you, He bore your infirmities and carried your sicknesses, that by His stripes you are healed!

Expect to live in health. And if you are sick, accept Him as your Healer. Be thoroughly convinced from Scripture that it is God's purpose to heal you and cause you to prosper. For you cannot be in faith for your healing if you do not know it is His purpose to heal you.

He wants to use you as an instrument of healing others. Believers 'will place their hands on sick people and they will recover'.

> As you go, preach this message: 'The kingdom of heaven is near.' Heal the sick, raise the dead, cleanse those who have leprosy, drive out demons. Freely you have received, freely give. (Matthew 10:7–8)

Jesus says that as a believer 'you will do the same things' that He has done. **Like Him, you need to follow the leading of the Holy Spirit, speaking the words He gives you to speak, doing the things He shows you to do. When you obey Him, He will use you to bless others and glorify the Father!**

The power and authority to heal that Jesus gives His friends are to be used in the way He directs. We are not free to do whatever we think right. When praying with others, it is important to be sensitive to the Holy Spirit, so that we know what and how to pray. Jesus often prayed in completely different ways for the same need. For example, he healed blindness using four different methods! And He usually drew out a response of faith before He prayed at all!

Prayer: *Lord Jesus, thank you for being my healer, my health and my salvation.*

Jesus Takes the Burdens of His Friends

> Come to me, all you who are weary and burdened, and
> I will give you rest. Take my yoke upon you and learn
> from me, for I am gentle and humble in heart, and you
> will find rest for your souls. For my yoke is easy and
> my burden is light. (Matthew 11:28–30)

Come to me is a personal invitation. Jesus does not say,
'come to a service', or 'come to church'; He says 'Come to
me.' He draws people into this personal bond with Himself. And this is not an exclusive call to spiritually mature
people. It is addressed to **all** who are weary and burdened.

There are times when we all fall into this category. Sometimes we are weary with ourselves, with others, or with
our circumstances. Sometimes we feel burdened by the
pressures and problems we face, at home, in our work or in
our finances. Sometimes we feel that others put us under
pressure and cause us to feel burdened. Sometimes we can
be weary and burdened because of pain and sickness.
Things can reach a point where we feel unable to cope.

It is often at such times that people initially turn to the
Lord and are born again. Having tried to live without Jesus,
they come to recognize their need of Him. However, these
are words that are not addressed exclusively to those outside a relationship with Jesus. It is certainly possible to
belong to Him, to know you are a child of God, and still be
burdened and weary. You may even have grown weary
doing the Lord's work!

Whatever your circumstances, the Lord's words are relevant: 'Come to **Me**!'

When you walk close to Jesus, it is automatic to turn to Him in any need or when feeling under pressure. You don't turn to others instead of Him. It is not counselling you want, for you know He alone is the answer to your need. **There is no substitute for dealing directly with the Lord.**

Jesus is with you, always available and ready to help when you are weary and burdened. He does not say, 'Go to a counsellor'; He says, 'Come to **Me**.' Every time you turn to Him your relationship with Jesus is strengthened. You do not grow by using others as substitutes!

This is not only a matter of obedience; it is also a question of faith! You will turn to others only if you do not believe that by turning to Jesus you will find the necessary help and strength. **When you turn to Him and put your faith in Him, you will receive much better answers than you could possibly receive from anyone else!**

Does this mean there is no case in asking for the support of others when in difficult circumstances? Not at all! As part of the Body of Christ you are to bear the burdens of others and allow them to help you as well. Sometimes it is our pride that keeps us from allowing others to help us! Jesus also tells us that if two agree together in prayer, their Father in heaven will answer them!

However, this is not using others in place of faith in Jesus, but to agree with you in your faith! Together you respond to Jesus's invitation: 'Come to **Me**.'

The fact that He addresses all those who are weary and burdened is evidence that He wants to be involved in every aspect of our lives. He is concerned for the weary and burdened to such an extent that He wants to carry their burdens, to take the pressure that is causing them to feel the way they do.

Some allow their problems to drive them away from God. This is exactly what the devil wants. He suggests that Jesus could not possibly love you if you are allowed to suffer in such a way, or have such problems. He omits to say that he is often the cause of the problem, which he wants to use to try to drive a wedge between you and Jesus!

Jesus does not promise that His followers will be cushioned from the pressures of the world in which they live. On the contrary, He says that in the world they will have tribulation! Often the most difficult problems to cope with come from those within the Church. This should not surprise us. Just because people are within the Church does not mean that they live close to Jesus or walk as His friends. There will be worldliness in the Church if members are living worldly lives. The flesh is always at odds with the Spirit, no matter through whom fleshly attitudes are expressed!

You can feel more deeply hurt, though, when your problems are caused by other believers, who should be committed to love you!

Jesus's greatest opposition came from the Pharisees. He could see through their hypocrisy. They were devoted to their outward religious performances while their hearts were far from God. Consequently, they rejected Jesus and the things of the Spirit, preferring instead to put their faith in their religious practices, thinking that by strictly observing these they could find favour with God.

Jesus's invitation and command is simple: 'Come to me.' These words are even addressed to those who have grown weary of religion and feel burdened by the legalistic practices to which they have been accustomed. Where there is a lack of faith, you will find a mixture of law and disobedience to God's Word.

To those who come, Jesus gives this wonderful promise, 'And I will give you rest.' He will give you rest from all those things that have caused you to be weary and burdened, whether pressures of the world, oppression from the enemy, hurt caused by others, the bondage of religious legalism, sickness **or any kind of need.**

Jesus does not say that others will give you rest or will be the solution to your situation or the way in which you feel. He says that **He will give you rest.**

Prayer: *Lord Jesus, thank you for always being with me, ready to help.*

🕉

Forty-Two

五夕

Jesus Is Yoked with His Friends

Take my yoke upon you and learn from me.
(Matthew 11:29)

A yoke is a bar that goes across the shoulders of two
animals so that they can work together using their combined strength. Jesus invites you, or any who are weary or
burdened, to be yoked together with Him.

Jesus says: 'Take **my** yoke.' What yoke does Jesus have?

During His time on earth, Jesus lived 'yoked' to the
Father. The 'yoke' that bound them together was love. Because of His love for His Father, Jesus did what His Father
wanted; He obeyed Him in all respects. The 'yoke', then,
was one of loving obedience.

If Jesus had chosen to disobey His Father, He would
have thrown off that yoke. Then He would not have been
able to do anything, for He said that He could do nothing
by Himself. **While yoked with the Father, He could
speak His words and perform His works.**

Jesus invites you to take His yoke upon yourself. He asks
you to choose to be yoked with Him in love. He will not
force His yoke upon you; you have to take it upon yourself,
the yoke of loving obedience. You may have to bend your
stiff neck to what the Lord wants of you, to submit to His
yoke; but He has your best interests at heart!

Your independence is the issue at stake. Many who acknowledge the Lordship of Jesus Christ in their lives still

want to keep a measure of independence, although they may not readily acknowledge this to be the case. You may feel you want to be yoked to Jesus when you have a desperate need, but that you would like to throw off that yoke when it suits you!

When two friends walk together, they decide by mutual agreement where they will go together and what they will do together. As friends of Jesus, yoked together with Him, the situation is different. **He does not want to walk with you in your ways; He wants you to walk with Him in His ways.** Neither does He want you to throw off that yoke when it suits you. That will only lead to becoming weary and burdened again!

To be yoked with Jesus means you stand shoulder to shoulder with Him. You no longer make the plans as to where to go and what to do. Like Jesus in His desire to please the Father, you choose to please Him by going the way He decides, doing the things He leads you to do.

However, because the yoke is one of love, the Lord will not prevent you from throwing it off whenever you choose. If you do, you will get yourself into trouble! If you cast off the restraints that are put on the flesh when yoked with Jesus, you will begin to indulge yourself in ways that don't please Him. To cast off the yoke is to be disobedient, and disobedience always leads to tension in your relationship with Jesus, a certain distancing of yourself from Him and His purposes. To cast off the yoke is an act of independence, and indicates you intend to trust in yourself, instead of in Jesus.

This inevitably spells trouble, although you may not recognize this immediately, because the negative results sometimes take a little time to become apparent. **It is**

wiser to humble ourselves under the mighty hand of God and submit to Jesus's yoke. Then He is able to raise us up!

Prayer: *Lord Jesus, I choose to be yoked with you.*

ॐ

Jesus Gives His Friends Rest

Come to me, all you who are weary and burdened, and
I will give you rest. (Matthew 11:25)

It is not a burden to be yoked with Jesus. The very opposite is the case, for this is the way in which He will give you
rest! Your flesh will consider it a burden to be yoked with
Jesus, for then you will not have your own way! Some want
the benefits of His friendship, blessings and inheritance;
but on their own terms, not His – without being yoked
to Jesus!

To refuse His yoke is likely to increase the pressure in
your life, rather than relieve it. Sin is the greatest pressure
you experience, and causes more destruction than anything else in your life. You do more damage to yourself
through sin than others do to you through hurt!

To be yoked with Jesus means you will benefit in four
ways: **You will learn from Him, you will experience His
gentleness, you will feel His humility of heart, and you
will find rest for your soul!**

Jesus suffered constant rejection and persecution, especially from those who professed legalistic religion. His
friends often failed Him and even deserted Him in His
greatest hour of need. Yet He was able to overcome every
difficulty because He yoked Himself voluntarily to the
Father.

When you choose to be yoked with Jesus, He is able to

carry you through the trials and difficulties you face. Being yoked with His Father meant that Jesus could reveal His Father's love and power. **The same will be true for you. And just as the Father was pleased with His Son, so Jesus will be pleased with you because you choose to remain yoked with Him in love, dependent on Him instead of being wilful and independent!**

Being yoked with the Father enabled Jesus to live the life of the heavenly Kingdom on earth. Yoked to Jesus, you can expect His life, love and power will be expressed in your life. And He will keep you in His peace that passes all understanding!

To the natural mind, to be yoked speaks of a lack of freedom, of bondage even. **To be in bondage to Jesus is complete freedom!** To refuse to be yoked with Jesus leaves you in bondage to self, an indication that you still want self to be on the throne of your life, or at least to share the throne with Jesus.

You are not yoked with one who wants to judge you, but with one who is gentle! You need gentleness when you feel weary and burdened. You want someone who understands you and the situation you are in. Jesus does not lecture you when you turn to Him – He helps you.

Cast **all** your burdens on the Lord, for He cares for you. To hold on to any of your problems is to be disobedient. **You are yoked with Him; He is your partner in everything, and is able to take the strain, no matter what the situation.** By learning to trust the Lord in small things, you will learn to trust Him for major problems. This is the first benefit.

The second benefit is that Jesus expresses His love for you with great gentleness. He does not judge you for getting into a situation of need; He wants to help you out of your predicament. Jesus forgave the woman caught in adultery instead of condemning her. The father welcomed back the prodigal son instead of reading the riot act for wasting his inheritance!

When a child is in need, a loving parent will lavish the tender care on him or her that the situation demands. Do you imagine that your heavenly Father would be less loving, gentle, tender or kind with any of His children in need?

He knows when you need to be confronted with your rebellion, disobedience or unbelief. Even then He will not do this in a way that will devastate you. He doesn't want to place burdens on you; He wants to lift them from you. He knows also when you simply need His tender, loving care to encourage and sustain you. **He is gentle with you!**

Prayer: *Lord Jesus, thank you that you take the strain and give me rest.*

☙

Jesus Humbly Serves His Friends

Take my yoke upon you and learn from me, for I am
gentle and humble in heart. (Matthew 11:29)

Many Christians long to see more of God's power in their
lives. However, it is not the receiving of God's power that
causes us to live in victory, but the demonstration of that
power. **Jesus shows us that it is important to walk in
humble submission to the Father if His power is going
to be demonstrated in our lives.** This is the third benefit.

Anyone who has tried to be humble knows what an im-
possible task this is if we attempt it in our own strength!
Humility before others comes from humility before God.
**True humility flows from being yoked with the One
who is humble of heart.** Then we will have hearts after
His own heart!

Jesus expressed humility in coming to earth as the willing servant of all. Even though the Son of God, He lived as
a servant, and spent His entire ministry serving those
around Him. **Today He wants to serve you; He still has
the same loving, humble, servant heart!**

Pride is the biggest enemy for every believer. Pride lies
behind unbelief and any other way in which we resist the
purposes of God. Pride gives the devil opportunity to deceive, and causes us to imagine we can manage on our
own, without being yoked to Jesus.

Pride causes some to think they do not have to live as

friends of Jesus, that they can follow Him without having to deny themselves and willingly take up whatever cross He places before them. Pride lies behind every sinful and rebellious attitude on to which we cling. Pride is expressed in stubbornly refusing to repent and submit ourselves to Jesus.

True humility is to acknowledge that apart from Christ you can do nothing; you do not attempt to do things apart from Him, but in unison with Him. You live by faith in the Son of God, then all things become possible for you. So humility is a key to the release of God's power in your life!

Jesus would not have taken all your sickness upon Himself when He went to the cross unless it was God's purpose to heal you. Neither would He have told His followers to speak to mountains and command them to be moved, unless it was His intention to see the problems dealt with. He invites the weary and burdened to come and be yoked with Him because He wants to set them free, not to see them suffering under the burdens of the world, the flesh and the devil!

The Roman centurion understood that he could command the soldiers under him because he was obedient to those over him. If he was insubordinate, his authority would have been taken from him.

He saw the authority with which Jesus taught and acted. So much so, that he perceived that Jesus would only have to speak a word of command and his servant would be healed. There was no need for Jesus to come to his house to effect the healing. This is faith indeed. **Jesus could exercise such authority because He was submitted totally to the authority of His Father. He lived 'yoked' to His**

Father and so God's power could be manifested in wonderful ways in His ministry.

True humility, combined with faith, will lead to
demonstrations of God's power in your life. Staying
yoked with Jesus helps you stay in that place of humble
submission to Him and to His purposes, just as Jesus
remained humbly yoked to His Father.

Prayer: *Lord Jesus, apart from you I can do nothing.*

૩ℛ

Forty-Five

༕ལ

Jesus Gives His Friends Peace

For he himself is our peace. (Ephesians 2:14)

The fourth benefit Jesus mentions from being yoked together with Him, is that 'you will find rest for your souls'.
You will be at peace with God when you are in submission
to Jesus; but there will be tension when you persist stubbornly in demanding your own will instead of His.

There are three main areas to your soul life: your mind
or intellect, your emotions or feelings, and your will or
your ability to make choices.

**You have peace with the Lord when you submit your
thinking to His,** your understanding to His understanding
which is so much higher than your own! To be yoked with
Jesus is to be close to Him in His thinking. You begin to see
things as He sees them, to understand them as He does.

Most of us value our own opinions and ideas very highly,
so much so that we want to impress them on other people,
especially if we consider them to have inferior understanding!

You can choose to throw off the yoke of love at any
moment by simply disagreeing with Jesus, choosing your
thoughts above His and thus acting in disobedience. To
obey Jesus is to obey what He says, not your own ideas of
what His will should be!

Not only is it easy to believe your own thoughts rather
than those of Jesus; it is easier still to believe your own

feelings or emotions rather than the revelation of truth the Lord has given us in His Word. This is an area that is a real battleground for many believers; they live as victims of their feelings, instead of victors over their feelings.

We want to be free of emotional turmoil and to be at peace. Those who try to attain this without dependence on Jesus go from one crisis to another. God tells us to rejoice in all circumstances because this is His will for us in Christ Jesus. Unwillingness to do this, which is disobedience to God's Word and will, is usually the fruit of believing feelings rather than the truth.

Praise and thanksgiving direct our focus to Jesus, to His presence with us, no matter what the situation. If our focus is on Him, we begin to see our problems and situations in a different light, from a better perspective. We know in our minds that nothing is impossible for God, that no situation is beyond His power. Yet we can stubbornly refuse to submit ourselves to Him because we are full of self-pity, or even anger, because of the circumstances we have to face.

To refuse to rejoice in the Lord is tantamount to blaming Him for the situation, to question His love for us because things have become difficult.

Faith looks at the circumstances very differently. Faith turns to Him, trusts Him and knows that He will be faithful in answering the cry of our hearts, no matter how desperate things may appear to be.

A friend of Jesus will look to Him for friendship when it matters most, not be resentful, or imagine He does not care or is totally uninvolved with us in the problem. You cannot express faith in Jesus to resolve a situation if you blame Him for it, or imagine it is His will for you.

You will not have the faith to remove mountains if you

believe that God intends you to have them! Jesus would not have told us to speak to mountains and command them to be moved if He intended us to be stuck with them!

Feelings cannot change a situation, but God can; and when you trust Him to do so, your feelings will change! **Instead of listening to your feelings, listen to what the Lord says in His Word.**

When you rejoice and give thanks you are expressing faith in God above your own thinking and feelings. You choose to do this. You submit your will to His. You choose His thoughts above your own. You choose obedience to His will and His Word above your own feelings.

Stubborn refusal to do this is indicative of the fact that your will is not submitted to His, certainly not in those circumstances, or at that time. Even when you need the Lord to act to change things, you will often find He does nothing until you come to a place of obedience. While you stubbornly refuse to rejoice or be thankful, it seems that there is little or no help forthcoming.

Nobody pretends it is always easy to put the Lord's Word into operation. The fact that it is difficult does not mean you have the right to try to create any easier solution of your own. Those alternatives will not work!

Obedience is not only doing what the Lord tells you to do in His Word, but doing it with the right attitude, rather than with bad grace or resentment. True submission admits that God's ways are always best and are just, and that He is at hand to bless, help, heal, deliver, give or do whatever is necessary! He will work according to His ways, not your ways. The outcome of all this is rest for your soul.

As your Friend, Jesus is always with you, always at hand, always ready to help, willing you to lay hold by

faith of all the resources He makes available to you. Yet, at the same time, He makes it clear that being yoked with Him, you will proceed according to His ways, not yours. He will not submit to you – you are to submit to Him. He is the Lord, not you.

His yoke is easy and His burden is light!

Prayer: *Lord Jesus, thank you for your peace.*

5♫

Forty-Six

Friends Obey Jesus

> Whoever has my commands and obeys them, he is the one who loves me. (John 14:21)

> If anyone loves me, he will obey my teaching. My Father will love him, and we will come to him and make our home with him. (John 14:23)

> If you obey my commands, you will remain in my love, just as I have obeyed my Father's commands and remain in his love. (John 15:10)

Jesus puts His love in your heart to create in you the desire to obey Him, to have a heart after His own heart. Then you will be prepared to face whatever cost may be involved in following Jesus. Obedience, Jesus says, is the outworking of your love for Him. This must mean that disobedience is the evidence of a lack of love, that you have chosen to please self instead of pleasing Him or others.

This love of self is the greatest hindrance to your Christian walk. You have been crucified with Christ and raised to a new life in Him! You have no identity or purpose apart from Him. To say that you belong to Him and still live for yourself is a contradiction in terms. You cannot be a witness for Jesus Christ in the world if you live as the world lives, but only if you demonstrate the new life that you have in Him.

Obedience draws you closer to Jesus; deliberate disobedience separates you from Him. You cannot walk with Him while disobeying Him. Darkness and light cannot have fellowship together.

God's command is to love Him with **all** your heart, **all** your mind, **all** your soul and **all** your strength. If you were asked whether you do that, you would probably answer truthfully that you love Him with some of your heart, some of your mind, some of your soul and some of your strength. You probably see readily that there is too much self-love, too many thoughts and desires centred on pleasing self. Decisions are often based on what you want, rather than on what Jesus wants for you.

Could things ever be different? Most definitely! Have you ever decided to love Jesus with all your heart, mind, soul and strength? Have you cried out to God and prayed earnestly that He will enable you to live in such a way because you desire so strongly to love Him whole-heartedly? Have you thought it possible?

Fervent prayer will be necessary, but it must be prayer with faith. Earnest prayer comes from your heart and touches the Lord's heart, convincing Him that you are serious. But you also believe He will answer you and enable you to love Him beyond your present capacity. Such prayer is not the result of a passing fancy. It comes from a deep heart longing.

Jesus has never compromised His love for you, and He wants no compromise in your love for Him. **No matter what your position, ministry, calling, job or profession, it is God's will for you to love Him with all your might.**

He longs for your fellowship, to be close to you, to help and provide for you. Are you hungry for Him? Do you want to walk close to Him, knowing His heart and doing His will? If so, never tire of telling Him that you love Him.

Rejoice in every opportunity He gives you to serve Him by loving others. At the same time realize how deeply He appreciates you and loves to meet with you, drawing you into ever fresh revelations of His love for you! **Believe that your love for Him will continue to increase!**

Prayer: *Lord Jesus, I want to love you with all my heart, mind, soul and strength.*

5♫

Friends Love Other Friends

> A new command I give you: Love one another. As I
> have loved you, so must you love one another. By this
> all men will know that you are my disciples, if you love
> one another. (John 13:34–35)

> My command is this: love each other as I have loved
> you. Greater love has no man than this, that he lay
> down his life for his friends. (John 15:12–13)

John, the apostle, was present when Jesus spoke these
words. He wrote his First Epistle some fifty years later, after
a long period of ministry during which he had seen these
principles in action! He says clearly that we demonstrate
our love for Jesus by loving others; for we cannot love God
without loving our brethren. To love the Father is to love
His children as well. If we see a brother in need and close
our hearts to him, the love of God cannot be in us. Anyone
who says he loves God but does not love his brother, is de-
ceived; he is a liar and the truth is not in him.

This is strong language! John obviously did not like
super-spirituality. It shows us how contradictory it is when
people have the right language but live in a different way. If
you have a heart of love, you will love Jesus, other Christians and anyone whom the Lord places before you. You
will have a particular care for the lost, the poor and the
needy, as Jesus Himself demonstrated in His life on earth.
You will love because you have a heart of love.

Living a life of love is not an option for Christians. Jesus says: 'You **must** love one another.' You are to do good to all men, but especially to those who are of the household of faith. When Christians love one another they demonstrate to the world the reality of God's love. They will not convince the world of the truth of the Gospel without demonstrating the life of which the Gospel speaks.

The only way to love Jesus is to obey Him. The only way to obey Him is to love others. He gives you the anointing to do this, but the anointing does not force you to be obedient. You still have to choose to use this anointing to love others as Jesus loves you.

Friends of Jesus are to love other friends, even to the point of laying your life down for them. What does this mean in practice? **It involves pleasing others before yourself; being willing to love and serve other brethren, regardless of the cost to you.** Like Jesus, you need a servant heart!

As you live in fellowship with Jesus, His love will flow out of you to bless others. This is the glorious consequence of being a friend of Jesus.

Prayer: *Lord Jesus, thank you for enabling me to love others*
as you have loved me.

ϽꞀ

Forty-Eight

🔊

Friends Bear Fruit

> You did not choose me, but I chose you and appointed
> you to go and bear fruit – fruit that will last. Then the
> Father will give whatever you ask in my name.
> (John 15:16)

> This is to my Father's glory, that you bear much fruit,
> showing yourselves to be my disciples. (John 15:8)

> No branch can bear fruit by itself; it must remain in
> the vine. Neither can you bear fruit unless you remain
> in me. (John 15:4)

> If a man remains in me and I in him, he will bear much
> fruit; apart from me you can do nothing. (John 15:5)

The Father has taken you out of the wild vine of the world
and grafted you into the true Vine, Jesus. The purpose of
every branch is to bear fruit by living in Him. No branch
can bear fruit independently of Him.

The fruit is not for the benefit of the branch. The
Father is the Vinedresser, and He is allowed to gather the
fruit produced in your life and give it to whomsoever He
pleases. He will cause others to pick and 'eat' the fruit you
produce. You should have no complaints about this because you did not produce this fruit for your own glory or
satisfaction, but for His glory. He has the right to do with
it as He pleases!

There may be occasions when the Lord sends people

you find difficult to receive the fruit of your love. It is not for you to say: 'Not that one, Lord,' or 'I don't like him,' or 'I haven't paid the cost for someone like her!'

Have you ever seen a branch eat its own fruit? Obviously not! If you are to rejoice always and give thanks in all circumstances, then you will rejoice in the ways in which the Lord chooses to use you, and give thanks for all those He gives you to love!

You can only be fruitful by abiding or remaining in the Vine. By living close to Jesus, the bearing of fruit will be inevitable. **Love will inevitably produce the fruit of love!**

You will not have to keep looking at yourself, anxious to know whether you are being fruitful. Because of the love the Lord places in your heart, you will welcome the opportunities He provides for you to serve and give to others.

You will want to reach out to others, overcoming any natural reluctance or fears you may have, even though you will sometimes make yourself vulnerable to rejection. Every day you will have to make decisions to deny yourself in order to love and serve others.

Sometimes your love may be rejected. At other times people will take you for granted or misunderstand your motives. All these things happened to Jesus, and He says that others will treat you in the same way as they treated Him. **All that matters is that you have obeyed the Lord, and He will bless you for your obedience.**

At other times people will appreciate your loving service and care, even though some may not know how to express their thankfulness. It is good and encouraging to be appreciated, but this is not your motive in loving others. It is enough to know that Jesus appreciates you and is pleased you obeyed Him. He promises you a rich reward in heaven because you glorify the Father by the fruit you produce.

Whatever you do to the least of Jesus's brothers, you do to Him. And what you do to Jesus, you do to the Father! When Jesus spoke of the sheep and goats, it is clear that the righteous were rewarded for their loving care of others. Here Jesus does not put the emphasis on healing the sick, but visiting them. He does not speak of releasing the captives, but of caring for them!

Through faith you become part of God's eternal Kingdom. Your love determines your reward in this Kingdom!

Prayer: *Lord Jesus, I want to bear much fruit for your Father's glory.*

🙠

Forty-Nine

Friends Receive Answers to Prayer

> If you remain in me and my words remain in you, ask whatever you wish, and it will be given you. (John 15:7)

> I tell you the truth, my Father will give you whatever you ask in my name. Until now you have not asked for anything in my name. Ask and you will receive, and your joy will be complete. (John 16:23–24)

> And I will do whatever you ask in my name, so that the Son may bring glory to the Father. You may ask me for anything in my name, and I will do it. (John 14:13–14)

Abiding in Jesus will benefit you, as well as bearing fruit that glorifies the Father. Your confidence in prayer will increase. The greater your faith in His love, the easier it is to believe He will fulfil His promise and willingly give you whatever you ask.

There is no point in praying unless you expect the right answers which will resolve the situation. Jesus's promises are very clear. You can ask for anything in His name and He will give it to you.

To ask in the name of Jesus means more than using His name when you pray. **To pray in His name means you pray as He would in that situation: with His faith and expectancy, knowing the Father's love for you and His desire to answer you.** You are not speaking into some void, hoping someone is there who hears you! You pray before the throne of God, the place to which Jesus has given you access through the shedding of His blood.

> I tell you the truth, anyone who has faith in me will do
> what I have been doing. He will do even greater things
> than these, because I am going to the Father.
> (John 14:12)

**Just as the love of Jesus in you will produce the fruit of
love in your life, so faith in Him will produce the works
of faith.** It is certainly a challenge to hear Jesus tell us that
anyone who has faith in Him **will** do the same things that
He has done, and even greater things still.

**Jesus will continue to do His works on earth through
those who believe in Him.** Because He is the same yes-
terday, today and for ever, He will do the same works
through us today as He did in His manhood. This is amazing enough, but how could it be possible for us to do even
greater things than Jesus? Such a thought would seem
blasphemous if it had not come from the lips of Jesus
Himself.

Jesus does not say that the accumulated works of all
believers would be greater than what He was able to do as
an individual. He is speaking of every individual believer,
to '**anyone**' who has faith. '**He**' or she will do even greater
things.

During His ministry Jesus did not pray for people to receive the Holy Spirit. When He returned to the Father,
Jesus asked for the Holy Spirit to be poured out on whoever believed in Him. Until Jesus had returned to heaven,
and to the glory that was His rightful inheritance, His Spirit
could not come to live in His friends. Once they had received the glorified, victorious Spirit of Jesus, the greater
things could happen!

For God to come and live in someone is the greatest work of all, much greater than any healing or any other kind of miracle. Yet any believer who has himself received the Spirit is able to pray for others to receive this wonderful miracle! **The Lord has made it possible for you to impart this great blessing to others in His name.**

Prayer: *Lord Jesus, thanking you for the privilege of praying in your name.*

৵৹

Fifty

უ<u>ე</u>

Friends Do the Same as Jesus

The more you know of His compassion, the easier it will be to trust God to meet every need in your life, and enable you to be a channel of His grace to others. God's mercy moves Him to action.

> The Lord is gracious and compassionate, slow to anger and rich in love. The Lord is good to all; he has compassion on all he has made. (Psalm 145:8–9)

Jesus wants this to become a description of you – gracious, compassionate, slow to anger and rich in love. It is more blessed to give than to receive. You reap what you sow. In giving you are opening yourself to be able to receive all the Lord wants to give you in response to your prayer!

The Lord does not answer you regardless of other things in your life. 'If you live in me and my words live in you,' says Jesus, 'ask whatever you wish, and it will be given you.' As you live to give to others, you can be confident of His desire to give to you.

Everything Jesus did was for the glory of His Father. He will bless and anoint you for the same purpose. If you desire to be as fruitful as possible, you will see the need for the Lord to prune out of your heart and life everything that is a contradiction to love for Him, and which hinders you from loving others.

The Father prunes even the fruitful branches of the vine so that they become more fruitful still. He sees the greater ways in which He can use you to bless others, once He has dealt with more of the useless, fruitless parts of your life. **It is best to welcome the pruning, instead of trying to avoid it.** Pruning is often a painful process because usually the Lord confronts us with issues we would rather avoid. He knows we will be much purer when those issues are dealt with, and we will be able to be more effective in the ministries to which He has called us.

Jesus is love. If you are to do the same works, you will do the works of love and compassion as well as faith!

In compassion He forgave; **you are to forgive others.**

In compassion He pastored the people by teaching them the truth, because He saw they were as sheep without a shepherd. **You are to have a pastoral care and concern for others, wanting to see them set free by the power of His words of truth.**

In compassion He fed the multitude, even though it required a miracle to do so. And His word is still: **'You feed them.'**

In compassion He healed the sick. He looks on the sick with the same compassion today and promises that **the sick will be healed when believers lay hands on them!**

He is the Author and Perfecter of your faith; His power and authority can be revealed through you. Don't say that these things are beyond you and for the privileged few. Every believer is to obey every command given to the first disciples. **As a friend of Jesus you have His power and authority**

to speak and act in His name. He is with you always to encourage you, His Spirit within you to enable you! He will tell you what to do, and everything you do in obedience to Him will work!

Love is the most powerful form of evangelism. God can use you to love others into His Kingdom. You can take His compassion to any group of needy people, as the Spirit leads you. And you do not have to go alone. Many need the support of others; they are much more effective as team members than they would ever be on their own.

Friends of Jesus can go with the love and compassion of Jesus to visit the sick in hospitals, those in prison; they can feed the hungry, give hospitality to the destitute. They can care for those in retirement homes, seeking to bring them to a knowledge of Jesus's love before it is too late.

Groups of friends can go to the addicts and alcoholics, the desperate, the unmarried mothers, single-parent families, even the affluent who live in deception! **They do not go in judgement but in love and compassion, to serve and bless. They go in the name of Jesus.**

Prayer: *Lord Jesus, thank you that through faith in you, I can do the same things as you did.*

ℜℜ

Fifty-One

🔊

Friends Are Sent by Jesus

As you sent me into the world, I have sent them into the world. (John 17:18)

As the Father has sent me, I am sending you.
(John 20:21)

The Church is to fulfil the Great Commission, to continue Jesus's ministry in the world, to preach the Gospel of the Kingdom of God, to 'go and make disciples of all nations, baptizing them in the name of the Father and of the Son and of the Holy Spirit, and teaching them to obey everything I have commanded you. And surely I am with you always, to the very end of the age' (Matthew 28:19–20).

Christians need continual reminders that Jesus did not call them to a series of services, meetings or conferences, but to take His life and love out into the world as His witnesses. This is not a matter of preference or choice for believers. It is a command from God!

Services, meetings and conferences are times of receiving from the Lord to make you more effective in your ministry and witness. Every healing and blessing is not an end in itself, but is given for God's glory and to enable greater effectiveness in communicating the Gospel to others.

Jesus spent time teaching and training the disciples, not for their own edification, but to equip them for ministry to others. The Father had sent Jesus to live for others, to lay His life down for them in love. In the same way Jesus sends

His friends out into the world as His witnesses. They are to live for others and lay down their lives for them in love.

You are not called to be a witness to those who know Him, but to those who don't know Him. Those who know Him don't need that witness. They need teaching, building up and encouraging. In a court of law a witness is called to give evidence to those who are ignorant of the facts. Not everyone is an evangelist, but everyone is to be a witness!

When Christians want to share Jesus with others, He provides them with the opportunities to do so!

Those who are part of the five-fold ministry that God has given to His Church, have the specific task of preparing God's people to 'go' in the name of Jesus.

> It was he who gave some to be apostles, some to be prophets, some to be evangelists, and some to be pastors and teachers, to prepare God's people for works of service, so that the body of Christ may be built up …
> (Ephesians 4:11–12)

The purpose of all these ministries is to 'prepare God's people for works of service'. They are to motivate the whole Body of Christ to fruitful activity. These are equipping and building ministries.

These ministries are not functions to which different people are called; they are different anointings the Holy Spirit gives. There is the apostolic anointing, the prophetic anointing, the evangelist's anointing, the pastor's and teacher's anointings. The Church is not built up, nor are people equipped, when these positions are filled by people who lack the necessary anointing.

When leaders are anointed, those they lead will come

under their anointings and will be influenced by them. Something of those anointings will be imparted to enable them to fulfil their role as 'co-workers with Christ'.

Many leaders never face the implication to teach their people to do everything Jesus commanded those first disciples to do. If the whole Church was motivated in that way, it would be on fire with God's love and power, and the world would be far more profoundly affected by the Gospel!

The whole body is sent. Every believer is to be a witness. And those in leadership ministries are to see that the rest of the Body is equipped for the tasks to which the Lord has called His people.

Prayer: *Lord Jesus, thank you for calling me to be your witness.*

ॐ

144

Friends Have Jesus's Authority

> If you forgive anyone his sins, they are forgiven; if you
> do not forgive them, they are not forgiven. (John 20:23)

> He called his twelve disciples to him and gave them au-
> thority to drive out evil spirits and to heal every disease
> and sickness. (Matthew 10:1)

> I have given you authority ... to overcome all the power
> of the enemy; nothing will harm you. (Luke 10:19)

The Lord sends you out, not only with His love and power,
but also with His authority. **You have divine authority to do
whatever He tells you to do, for when you act in obedience to Him you are truly acting in His name.** Paul says:

> And whatever you do, whether in word or deed, do it all
> in the name of the Lord Jesus, giving thanks to God the
> Father through him. (Colossians 3:17)

To this you are called. It is a mistake to think that everything you do is done in the name of Jesus, or everything
you pray is prayed in His name! It would be completely
wrong to suggest that any sinful act or disobedience to His
Word could be done in the name of Jesus!

**You only act in His name when you do what He tells
you to do. You only speak in His name when you speak
what He tells you to say. You only pray in His name
when you pray in the Spirit, with faith and according to
His Word!**

As a believer, you have been given great authority by God. You have the authority to forgive, the authority to heal in His name, authority over all the works of the evil one. **To do everything in Jesus's name is to work on His behalf and with His authority. And the authority of His name is greater than of any other name!**

You do not have to ask Him if He wants you to do the things He has commanded you to do. You know He wants you to go in His name to love others, forgive them, serve them, be His witness, preach the good news of God's Kingdom and heal the sick. You only need to be sensitive to the leading of His Spirit so that, like Jesus, you go about these tasks in the right way. He will show you what to do, what to preach, how to minister His healing grace and power – and He will tell you when!

You have the authority of God Himself to do whatever He asks of you.

Prayer: *Lord Jesus, thank you for the authority you give to me to act in your name.*

Fifty-Three

Friends Have the Joy of the Lord

> I have told you this that my joy may be in you and that
> your joy may be full. (John 15:11)

Jesus wants His disciples to be full of joy, and He knows this is only possible through obedience to the Father. He endured the cross because of the joy that was set before Him. **Christians discover the great joy that comes from pleasing the Lord by fulfilling what He asks of them. Every expression of love and sacrifice brings joy, even if it is costly.**

And this joy is eternal. Jesus taught that those who use their talents to the full are invited to enter into the eternal joys of the Lord, whereas those who bury their gifts receive no reward!

To live to please yourself is self-defeating because it has the opposite effect. Pleasing the Lord causes true and lasting joy. To live as a friend of Jesus gives true and lasting joy!

Jesus places these things together:

a) The revelation of how greatly He loves you.
b) Obedience enables you to live in His love.
c) The result of this is to have Jesus's own joy in you, and for your joy to be full.
d) The obedience required is to love others.

There is an obvious sequence in Jesus's train of thought here. And the overall message is inescapable. The way to true, full and lasting joy is to obey Jesus by loving others, by living to serve rather than living for yourself.

This is diametrically opposed to the world's way of

thinking. So much in modern society is aimed at encouraging people to live for themselves and to indulge themselves!

The friends of Jesus have to stand firm against such values. They know that a life of giving enables them to enjoy God's blessings. As they give, so the Lord will give, 'a good measure, pressed down, shaken together and running over, will be poured into your lap. For with the measure you use, it will be measured to you' (Luke 6:38).

The Lord loves a joyful giver. And the result? His joy will increase. The Lord loves obedience. So submission to His will leads to joy. The Lord loves faith. He answers our prayers of faith so that our 'joy may be full'.

The Christian life is to be one of continual joy: Paul says: 'Rejoice in the Lord always. I say it again: Rejoice!' (Philippians 1:4). Because he or she rejoices in the Lord, the friend of Jesus rejoices in Him irrespective of circumstances! Circumstances will change, but the Lord is always the same, always worthy of our praise, always with us, always ready to answer the cry of our hearts! As the prophet says:

> Though the fig tree does not bud, and there are no grapes on the vines, though the olive crop fails and the fields produce no food, though there are no sheep in the pen and no cattle in the stalls, yet I will rejoice in the Lord, I will be joyful in God my Saviour. (Habakkuk 3:17–18)

In other words, even when the situation seems completely and utterly hopeless, still I will rejoice in the Lord! For only He is able to deliver me!

Prayer: *Lord Jesus, thank you for the joy that comes from obeying your will.*

Fifty-Four

Friends Have His Peace

Peace I leave with you; my peace I give you. I do not
give as the world gives. Do not let your hearts be trou-
bled and do not be afraid. (John 14:27)

Peace be with you! (John 20:21)

Jesus wants to impart His peace to you and keep you in
that peace. When He says, 'Peace be with you,' He is not
simply giving the disciples a greeting – He is actually imparting His peace to them!

Sickness is dis-ease. A lack of peace causes emotional
stress and is also behind many physical disorders. Doctors
estimate that at least 70 per cent of physical sickness is
psychosomatic, the result of the way mental stress and
tension have affected the body.

The Lord wants you to be healthy in both mind and
body. He did not create you to be sick! God did not give
you a spirit of fear, but 'a spirit of power, of love and self-
discipline' (2 Timothy 1:7).

Fear is the opposite of peace, and Jesus doesn't want
His friends sick in mind or body because of tension.
**Believers are to impart peace to others and can only
do that inasmuch as they allow Jesus to impart His peace
to them!** To receive that peace brings health and healing!

God's peace is not simply the absence of tension, turmoil
or fear. It is a positive attribute of God Himself. He is our
peace. When Jesus gave His peace to the disciples He imparted something of Himself to them.

Whenever they entered a house, Jesus taught the disciples to say 'Peace be on this house'. If they were received, the Lord's peace would descend on those who lived there. But if the disciples were rejected, that peace would descend on the disciples themselves.

The point is this. 'Peace be with you' is not simply a greeting, but a way of imparting peace. They were speaking words of peace. That peace had to go somewhere. If those to whom it was spoken did not receive it, then that peace would descend on those who spoke the greeting.

This demonstrates the power of the word whenever we speak it. As friends of Jesus we can receive the impartation of His life and peace through the words He speaks: 'Peace I leave with you; my peace I give to you.'

Whenever you are feeling under pressure, sit down for two or three minutes and allow your Friend, Jesus, to speak these words to you personally. Repeat them slowly again and again, aloud if you are able: 'Peace I leave with you; my peace I give to you.' See the effect this has as His peace comes over you.

Realize that God can use you to give His peace to others. Your words can impart blessing or curse. Both can flow from the same tongue. **As a friend of Jesus you want to impart words of life, of blessing and encouragement to others – words of peace. He sends you out with the Gospel of peace!**

Prayer: *Lord Jesus, thank you that I can impart the blessing of your peace to others.*

Fifty-Five

ॐ

Friends Are One with Each Other

I pray also for those who will believe in me through
their message, that all of them may be one, Father, just
as you are in me and I am in you. (John 17:21)

May they be brought to complete unity to let the world
know that you sent me and have loved them even as
you have loved me. (John 17:23)

Peace with God leads to peace with others. To be at one
with Him leads to unity with fellow believers. It was for
this unity that Jesus prayed, because He understood how
crucial it was to the whole cause of His Kingdom.

The world needs to see this unity. Sadly, it is more aware
of the things that divide Christians than of seeing a love
that transcends their differences and draws them together.
Jesus wants it to be obvious to the world that the Father
loves His modern disciples as much as He loves Jesus Himself. He wants believers to be filled with the Father's own
love for Jesus! What a prayer! **If they love Him with the
Father's love, Jesus knows they will also love one another. Then the world will believe!**

**You have within you the same love for Jesus that the
Father has, the love that the Holy Spirit has given you.**
That same love is in the other friends of Jesus. You may not
agree with them on every point of doctrine, or have the
same faith in the power of God's Word. You may have a
different style of worship or other ways of praying. None of

these differences should divide you from the unity that you have in Christ, as members of the one Church. For truly Jesus has only one Body consisting of all born-again believers.

The Lord wants you to recognize this unity of love, to affirm other believers, even when you do not agree with them. He hates to see pride and self-righteousness in any of His children, for these drive them apart. He wants them to recognize their unity in Christ, and to be prepared to pray and work together for the cause of His Kingdom.

So Jesus not only wants you to be His friends, but to recognize others who are His friends as members of the same family of believers. **No matter what your differences, you have the same Lord, the same Father, the same Friend and the same Holy Spirit living in you! To love God is to love His children also!**

Prayer: *Lord Jesus, thank you for the unity I have with other believers.*

🔊

The New Covenant

> Then he took the cup, saying, 'This cup is the new
> covenant in my blood, which is poured out for you.'
> (Luke 22:20)

Since His earliest dealings with man, God has chosen to relate to His people through a series of covenants. A covenant is an agreement made between two parties. Any covenant with God is not, of course, an agreement between two equal parties, for He is so much greater than those He has made.

God has never needed to relate to His people in a covenant relationship, but this is the way He has chosen to work. Jesus came to establish an entirely new covenant between His Father and those who believed in Him, different from what had been possible under the law given to Israel through Moses, generally known as the Old Covenant.

The New Covenant, or agreement, was sealed and ratified through the shedding of Jesus's blood. At the Last Supper, when Jesus took the cup and gave thanks to His Father, He said: 'This is my blood of the new covenant.' The sacrifice Jesus made for us on the cross enables us to be forgiven, accepted, made righteous, holy and one with Him. The law could accomplish none of these things!

Under the Old Covenant, Abraham and Moses related to the Lord as His friends. **Under the New Covenant, all who believe in Jesus can relate as friends.**

God is always faithful and keeps any agreement He makes. Under the Old Covenant, He remained faithful no matter how often Israel failed to honour her side of the agreement.

The Lord called Israel an adulterous wife because she so often forsook the covenant to obey the law God had given, and followed her own ways instead. Sometimes the people ignored Him altogether, even to the point of seeking after other gods. And yet, through His wonderful mercy, the Lord restored them again and again when they turned back to Him and embraced His covenant afresh.

The Lord envisaged not simply a covenant agreement; He wanted a covenant relationship: 'You will be my people and I will be your God.' This means a personal relationship expressed in personal commitment to one another.

Conscious that they live by grace and not by law, many Christians wrongly think there is nothing to bind them to the Lord in obedience. They want the benefits of His blood, but not to live in obedience. They need the Lord's mercy, but can fall into the error of believing their sin is not of any great significance as the Lord is so willing to forgive and restore His people.

He is always willing to forgive when we ask for His forgiveness. The effect of sin is always to separate man from God. Christians impress this truth on the unsaved. Sin does not become less important because a person is saved and has been introduced to the mercy of God! It is always disobedience to God's will and purpose.

It is difficult to live in close relationship with Him if we are walking in deliberate sin, for sin produces tension between the believer and his or her Lord. That tension is only removed through forgiveness. For this reason we are completely dependent on the blood of Jesus Christ to remove the guilt caused by sin and restore our relationship with God.

The power of that blood is so effective that God treats us, once forgiven, as if the sin had never taken place. He does not hold grudges, neither does He punish us. Even the punishment we deserve was carried by Jesus on the cross. Without the cross it would be impossible for us to be friends of Jesus!

However, this does not mean we can treat sin lightly. All sin is deeply offensive to God. If He were to treat us as we deserve, we would not be able to stand in His presence, even for a moment. He is holy, righteous, full of light and in Him there is no darkness at all. All sin is darkness, and Jesus came to eradicate such darkness. We are now the children of light, called to walk in the light. It is never the Lord's purpose for His children to walk in the darkness of sin.

The covenant relationship made possible by Jesus means that He now expects us to walk in the light as the children of light. In other words, we are to forsake sin and seek to please Him by living as His friends in loving obedience to Him. So the principle of the New Covenant is similar to all the previous covenants in the Bible. **We are to be His people, living in loving and faithful obedience to Him as our Lord and Master, our Friend and Brother. And He will be our God, fulfilling every promise He has made through His love and faithfulness.** God will fulfil His side of the agreement, and He expects us to do the same.

Prayer: *Lord Jesus, thank you for making me a part of your New Covenant.*

The Covenant of Love

Many Christians know that there is a New Covenant, but not all know what the substance of that covenant is, nor have they devoted themselves to the task of living out this agreement. **People will not set their hearts to keep an agreement with God unless they understand what that agreement involves, and unless they make a definite decision to keep it!**

God's grace is so amazing that He knows all that is imperfect about us, but still blesses us richly! This is not an excuse for us to treat His grace with contempt and think that sin doesn't matter. We need to set our hearts on pleasing Him by fulfilling the covenant He has established through Jesus.

The love that the Father places in us enables us to live according to the New Covenant and gives us the motivation to keep that covenant.

At the Last Supper, when He called the disciples His friends, Jesus told them what it means to be in a New Covenant relationship with Him:

As the Father has loved me, so have I loved you. Now remain in my love. If you obey my commands, you will remain in my love, just as I have obeyed my Father's commands and remain in his love. I have told you this so that my joy may be in you and that your joy may be

complete. My command is this: Love each other as I
have loved you. Greater love has no one than this, that
he lay down his life for his friends. You are my friends if
you do what I command. I no longer call you servants,
because a servant does not know his master's business.
Instead, I have called you friends, for everything that I
learned from my Father I have made known to you. You
did not choose me, but I chose you and appointed you
to go and bear fruit – fruit that will last. Then the Father
will give you whatever you ask in my name. This is my
command: Love each other. (John 15:9–17)

We have been speaking of this covenant love throughout
this book. Let us summarize the meaning of these words:

**The covenant relationship the Lord establishes with
His people is one of love.** The Father sent His Son to reveal the nature of His love for His people. Jesus was the
perfect human embodiment of God's love. He loves each
disciple in the same way that the Father loves Him.

**Because Jesus loves His disciples, He wants them to
live in His love.** Disciples are to abide in Jesus's love; they
are to remain in that love, live continuously in that love.
They are to live continuously in the revelation and reality
of His eternal and perfect love for them.

**Obedience enables the believer to live continually in
the reality of Jesus's powerful love.** Disobedience, therefore, prevents abiding in His love. We are not free to please
ourselves by doing whatever we fancy while claiming to
live in the love of God!

Obedience is not an option for Christians, but an ab-
solute necessity. Receiving the Father's love for the Son will
give you the desire to obey, but you still have to make the

right choices, putting that love into action. You still have to express that love, to abide and live continually in that love.

To live in the Father's love, Jesus had to obey His Father's commands. He could not reveal God's love to the world without living in that love Himself. Because Jesus loved the Father He obeyed Him and maintained His unity with Him. It was necessary for Jesus to obey the Father to maintain His relationship of love and unity with Him. **In the same way it is certainly necessary for us to maintain our relationship with the Lord through our obedience to what He asks of us!** This is not to be the slavish obedience of legalistically obeying written commands. Referring to the New Covenant, the Lord promised:

> I will put my law in their minds and write it on their hearts. I will be their God and they will be my people.
> (Jeremiah 31:33)

The Lord writes His commands on our hearts, not on tablets of stone. He is able to put within us the desire to obey Him out of love for Him, not out of slavish obedience.

As a result, His joy fills the life of those who live as His friends, who walk with Him in the way He sets before them. It is deeply satisfying to know you have pleased the Lord by fulfilling what He wants of you. When you cause the Lord joy, you share that joy with Him. If you are yoked with Jesus in loving obedience, your joy will be full or complete.

This is a much deeper joy than is produced by some passing experience, or from choosing to please yourself. When you gratify the flesh, you have pleased yourself but grieved the Spirit. As a result, there is no deep or lasting joy. When you please the Lord, you have been fruitful and have brought Him glory. The result is that your spirit can truly rejoice in Him.

You remain in Jesus's love by loving others in the same way as He loves you. What seems to be impossible is made possible through the love He gives you! What is impossible in your own strength becomes possible through faith in Him! All the resources of His Spirit are within you to enable you to love with His love. Do not expect failure. You know your own human love is weak, but His love in you is powerful. You will be able to love any the Lord asks you to love. What you could not do with your natural ability, you are able to do because of the supernatural anointing He has given you. This enables you to exercise patience beyond your natural ability; to show people love, compassion, mercy and grace that could only be the result of the Lord living out His life in you.

You no longer need to strive in your own strength to obey all the Lord wants us to be and to do; the Holy Spirit within you will express His life through you as you yield to Him. The secret is 'Christ in you, the hope of glory!'

The Lord requires your co-operation. He will not force you to obey Him. With a clean heart, filled with His love, you will want to serve others and give to them, just as the Lord has been so gracious to you!

Prayer: *Lord Jesus, I want to prove faithful in my covenant relationship with you.*

ॐ

🔊

Fifty-Eight

Friends Keep the Covenant

Dear friends, let us love one another, for love comes from God. Everyone who loves has been born of God and knows God. (1 John 4:7)

It is possible to sum up the message of John's First Epistle by saying that the only valid way of assessing your true relationship with the Lord is by looking at the way in which you relate to others. In your relationships with others, especially with other believers, you see a reflection of your relationship with God.

It is apparent, therefore, that some live in super-spiritual unreality. They have the right spiritual vocabulary, but not the right lifestyle. They say the right things, but make themselves scarce when there is work to be done. This is no way for true friends of Jesus to live. **Out of their love for Him, they will want to serve those He loves and for whom He gave His life.**

Jesus helps us to see what this means in practice. In loving us He had to lay down His life for us. **If we are to love in the same way, then we will have to lay down our lives for our friends**. Who are our friends? Not only those we choose to be close to, but all the other friends of Jesus, whoever they may be.

God's vision for His Church is a people of love, their love for one another being a witness to the world of the truth of the Gospel and a revelation of God's own heart. 'See how these Christians love one another!'

What does it mean to lay down your life for others? You live for them rather than for yourself. You put them first, being prepared to face whatever sacrifices are necessary in order to fulfil the demands of real love. Such love is certainly possible when the hearts of God's children are truly filled with His love, and when they devote themselves to a life of pleasing Him.

God does not want His Church to be 'meeting orientated', but 'love orientated'. When this is the case, believers want to love, serve and encourage other people. They see their call and mission in terms of reaching others, whether believers or unbelievers, with the love and the truth of Jesus Christ. It sounds a great concept to place others above yourself, until you face the reality of what is involved in practice! The love of Jesus in believers enables them to face great cost and often danger in order to serve others in His name.

To lay down your life for others is the greatest expression of love, Jesus says. This is not a lifestyle only for advanced disciples! New Christians live sacrificially for others when they see other believers around them living in such a way.

When people are converted, their concept of what it means to be a Christian in practice will, to a great extent, be determined by what they see rather than by what they are told. They look at others to see how to live out the Christian life. If they see it means attending the services, Bible study and prayer meetings, they will do this. If they see it means being not only a hearer but a doer of the Word, then they will set about living the Word. **If they see that to follow Christ means living a life of love, laying down your life for others, this is what they will do.**

Those who are His friends adopt this lifestyle! Do not be

discouraged if it seems that you have been a Christian for some time, with good intentions but without bearing much fruit. This can change rapidly. **See yourself as His friend, able to enjoy a close working relationship with Him as a 'fellow worker' with Christ, with His love within you!**

There is much to be done to spread the Gospel of God's love throughout the world, and Jesus has called you to be part of this work. There are to be no passengers in the Body of Christ. Everyone is called upon to work!

He does not want you to feel condemned to a life of useless and fruitless futility. It is the devil's lie to think that God could not use you in significant ways. Virtually every day you can express the love of Jesus in a variety of ways. He will show you what to do. **Jesus wants you to realize the glorious possibilities of what can be accomplished through your life.**

Prayer: *Lord Jesus, thank you for enabling me to live as your friend.*

🔊

The Vision

> May they be brought to complete unity to let the world
> know that you sent me and have loved them even as
> you have loved me. (John 17:23)

It has never been God's desire to have a Church that is divided, Christians at odds with one another, speaking against each other, competing with one another. He does not want a lukewarm Church full of compromise and worldliness. It was never His intention to have a hypocritical Church that preaches one thing while manifesting the very opposite.

Sadly this has often been a picture of the Church historically. All too often it is an accurate description of what is to be found today. This is not said critically, but with a heavy heart.

God loves His Church despite all her failings and inadequacies. Throughout the centuries He has never been without His witnesses, men and women of faith, who have held on to the Word of truth, lived lives of sacrificial love, and reached out to the world with the compassion and power of Christ. They have prayed with longing for God to revive His Church, to move through the nations with a powerful move of His Spirit to prepare for Jesus to come again in glory!

The fact that Jesus prays for unity that the world might believe shows how crucial this is to His purposes. It explains also why the devil is so intent on causing division.

Jesus's prayer will be answered! It is inconceivable that the Father would turn a deaf ear to His Son.

When we look at the Church today, we see many encouraging signs of spiritual life and activity the world over. However, there is still little sign of the unity for which Jesus prayed. Yes, this was His vision – **a Church full of love, where His friends lived for each other, affirming one another and standing together united in faith, His Body radiating His life, a witness of His love so that the world would know that He is God's Son.**

Jesus has never lost this vision. He believes it will surely come to pass. We need to unite our faith with His.

He is not satisfied with explanations about our invisible unity in Christ; He prays for a unity that will be **seen.** He is not content with talk that affirms there is more that unites us than divides us. He wants a Body in which the world can **see** His love and the unity that flows from it!

Is it really impossible that Christians the world over could unite in a real way? Could love for Jesus cause them to transcend the things that divide them so that they give a common witness to the world?

It must be possible or Jesus would not have prayed as He did. Certainly, only the Holy Spirit could bring such a vision to reality. Does this mean there is nothing we can do except sit back and wait for something to happen supernaturally, to draw Christians together suddenly in an amazing unity? There is nothing to suggest that God intends to do anything of that nature. How then will Jesus's prayer be answered?

The Holy Spirit will create initiatives which, when responded to by believers, will bring about the unity that Christ longs to see in His Body. One such initiative is the Friends of Jesus International!

Prayer: *Lord Jesus, please give me your love for your Church.*

Friends of Jesus International

Imagine thousands, tens of thousands, millions even, of Christians linked together across the world in a common bond of love and unity!

Impossible to achieve? Well, this is the vision the Lord has given me: in every nation where the name of Jesus is honoured, Christians living with Him as His friends, not in name only, but in reality; living and relating to Him as His friends.

There have been various organizations that God has raised up and used to bring either men or women together, but this vision is for the whole Body of Christ: Men and women living as Friends of Jesus; old and young living as Friends of Jesus; children living as Friends of Jesus.

The Lord does not want yet another organization, but Christians anointed by the Holy Spirit living in close relationship with Jesus and fulfilling His purposes for their lives. At the same time, they would acknowledge one another across differing church structures as those bound together in a covenant of love with Jesus and with one another.

The Purpose

This sounds like a good idea. But what would the purpose be? How could the **Friends of Jesus** serve the purposes of God's Kingdom?

1) **Friends of Jesus** promotes among believers the realization that it is possible to have such a relationship with Jesus Christ, to live and work with Him as a close friend.

2) People come to a greater understanding as to what it means to live as a **Friend of Jesus**.

3) By entering into a covenant to live as a **Friend of Jesus**, Christians are invited to embrace the commitment involved – the responsibilities as well as the privileges of being His friend.

4) Friends are supplied regularly with material to help them live as **Friends of Jesus**.

5) Friends can be linked together with other **Friends of Jesus** in their regions right across the spectrum of churches, thus expressing the unity for which Jesus prayed.

6) They can also be linked nationally and internationally by this common bond of love and commitment.

7) At regional, national and international meetings, Friends receive fresh anointing of love from the Holy Spirit to enable them to live as His friends.

8) Living as a **friend** enhances the believer's life spiritually and his/her relationships with others.

9) **Friends of Jesus** become more effective in their witness in the world.

10) **Friends of Jesus** are encouraged to bring their friends to meetings, that they may become **Friends of Jesus** themselves.

11) Promoting **Friends of Jesus** is a convenient way for church leaders to encourage their congregations to live in loving obedience to Jesus, and therefore to be enriched spiritually, both personally and as churches.

12) Material produced for leaders will help them draw their people into a closer relationship with Jesus and into a realistic commitment to live as His friends.

13) Material produced for teenagers helps them to face the particular challenges they face living as **Friends of Jesus** and being witnesses to their generation.

14) Material produced for children helps them to relate to Jesus as **friends**.

The Covenant

Below is the form of Covenant **Friends of Jesus** are asked to make. It is a précis of John 15:9–17.

> **Jesus Christ is my Saviour, my Lord and my Friend. He said:**

As the Father has loved me, so have I loved you. Now remain in my love.

If you obey my commands you will remain in my love.

I have told you this that my joy may be in you and that your joy may be complete.

My command is this: Love each other as I have loved you.

You are my friends if you do what I command.

I no longer call you servants ... Instead, I have called you friends.

You did not choose me, but I chose you and appointed you to go and bear fruit – fruit that will last.

Then the Father will give you whatever you ask in my name.

This is my command: Love each other.

By the grace of God and through the power of His Holy Spirit, I desire to live as a Friend of Jesus, and see these words fulfilled in my life.

You can be part of this worldwide movement that will bring Christians together in love and unity, seeking to live in this covenant relationship with Jesus and His friends. If you want to join us then please send your name and address to:

Friends of Jesus International
PO Box 95
Horsham
West Sussex RH13 5PX
UK
Tel/Fax: 01403 258040

Or e-mail us on: info@friends of jesus.net; or look at our web-site at: http:\\www.friendsofjesus.net.

Please state that you have read this book, and you will be sent further material to help you live as a **Friend of Jesus**, together with information about how you can be in contact with other **Friends of Jesus**, should you so desire.

I pray the Lord's blessing over your life as you seek to live out your call to be a **Friend of Jesus**.

Prayer: *Lord Jesus, by your grace and through the power of your Spirit, I desire to live as your friend and see your words fulfilled in my life.*